Contents

BLACK BEANS AND RICE

Servings: 10 | Prep: 5m | Cooks: 25m | Total: 30m

NUTRITION FACTS

Calories: 140 | Carbohydrates: 27.1g | Fat: 0.9g | Protein: 6.3g | Cholesterol: 0mg**INGREDIENTS**

- 1 teaspoon olive oil
- 1 1/2 cups low sodium, low fat vegetable broth
- 1 onion, chopped
- 1 teaspoon ground cumin
- 2 cloves garlic, minced
- 1/4 teaspoon cayenne pepper
- 3/4 cup uncooked white rice
- 3 1/2 cups canned black beans, drained

DIRECTIONS

1. In a stockpot over medium-high heat, heat the oil. Add the onion and garlic and saute for 4 minutes. Add the rice and saute for 2 minutes.
2. Add the vegetable broth, bring to a boil, cover and lower the heat and cook for 20 minutes. Add the spices and black beans.

SLOW COOKER CHICKEN POT PIE STEW

Servings: 16 | Prep: 20m | Cooks: 6h | Total: 6h20m

NUTRITION FACTS

Calories: 263 | Carbohydrates: 33.7g | Fat: 6.9g | Protein: 17.1g | Cholesterol: 37mg

INGREDIENTS

- 4 large skinless, boneless chicken breast halves, cut into cubes
- 6 cubes chicken bouillon
- 10 medium red potatoes, quartered
- 2 teaspoons garlic salt
- 1 (8 ounce) package baby carrots
- 1 teaspoon celery salt
- 1 cup chopped celery
- 1 tablespoon ground black pepper
- 2 (26 ounce) cans condensed cream of chicken soup
- 1 (16 ounce) bag frozen mixed vegetables

DIRECTIONS

1. Combine the chicken, potatoes, carrots, celery, chicken soup, chicken bouillon, garlic salt, celery salt, and black pepper in a slow cooker; cook on High for 5 hours.
2. Stir the frozen mixed vegetables into the slow cooker, and cook 1 hour more.

AMAZING WHOLE WHEAT PIZZA CRUST
Servings: 10 | Prep: 25m | Cooks: 20m | Total: 2h45m

NUTRITION FACTS

Calories: 167 | Carbohydrates: 32.6g | Fat: 2g | Protein: 5.7g | Cholesterol: 0mg

INGREDIENTS

- 1 teaspoon white sugar
- 1 teaspoon salt
- 1 1/2 cups warm water (110 degrees F/45 degrees C)
- 2 cups whole wheat flour
- 1 tablespoon active dry yeast
- 1 1/2 cups all-purpose flour
- 1 tablespoon olive oil

DIRECTIONS

1. In a large bowl, dissolve sugar in warm water. Sprinkle yeast over the top, and let stand for about 10 minutes, until foamy.
2. Stir the olive oil and salt into the yeast mixture, then mix in the whole wheat flour and 1 cup of the all-purpose flour until dough starts to come together. Tip dough out onto a surface floured with the remaining all-purpose flour, and knead until all of the flour has been absorbed, and the ball of dough becomes smooth, about 10 minutes. Place dough in an oiled bowl, and turn to coat the surface. Cover loosely with a towel, and let stand in a warm place until doubled in size, about 1 hour.
3. When the dough is doubled, tip the dough out onto a lightly floured surface, and divide into 2 pieces for 2 thin crust, or leave whole to make one thick crust. Form into a tight ball. Let rise for about 45 minutes, until doubled.
4. Preheat the oven to 425 degrees F (220 degrees C). Roll a ball of dough with a rolling pin until it will not stretch any further. Then, drape it over both of your fists, and gently pull the edges outward, while rotating the crust. When the circle has reached the desired size, place on a well oiled pizza pan. Top pizza with your favorite toppings, such as sauce, cheese, meats, or vegetables.
5. Bake for 16 to 20 minutes (depending on thickness) in the preheated oven, until the crust is crisp and golden at the edges, and cheese is melted on the top.

LOW-FAT BLUEBERRY BRAN MUFFINS
Servings: 12 | Prep: 15m | Cooks: 20m | Total: 35m

NUTRITION FACTS

Calories: 123 | Carbohydrates: 28.3g | Fat: 0.9g | Protein: 3.7g | Cholesterol: 16mg

INGREDIENTS

- 1 1/2 cups wheat bran
- 1/2 cup all-purpose flour
- 1 cup nonfat milk
- 1/2 cup whole wheat flour
- 1/2 cup unsweetened applesauce
- 1 teaspoon baking soda
- 1 egg
- 1 teaspoon baking powder
- 2/3 cup brown sugar
- 1/2 teaspoon salt
- 1/2 teaspoon vanilla extract
- 1 cup blueberries

DIRECTIONS

1. Preheat oven to 375 degrees F (190 degrees C). Grease muffin cups or use paper muffin liners. Mix together wheat bran and milk, and let stand for 10 minutes.
2. In a large bowl, mix together applesauce, egg, brown sugar, and vanilla. Beat in bran mixture. Sift together all-purpose flour, whole wheat flour, baking soda, baking powder, and salt. Stir into bran mixture until just blended. Fold in blueberries. Scoop into muffin cups.
3. Bake in preheated oven for 15 to 20 minutes, or until tops spring back when lightly tapped.

FANTASTIC BLACK BEAN CHILI
Servings: 6 | Prep: 20m | Cooks: 1h15m | Total: 1h35m

NUTRITION FACTS

Calories: 366 | Carbohydrates: 44.1g | Fat: 9.2g | Protein: 29.6g | Cholesterol: 56mg

INGREDIENTS

- 1 tablespoon vegetable oil
- 1 (14.5 ounce) can crushed tomatoes
- 1 onion, diced
- 1 1/2 tablespoons chili powder
- 2 cloves garlic, minced
- 1 tablespoon dried oregano
- 1 pound ground turkey
- 1 tablespoon dried basil leaves
- 3 (15 ounce) cans black beans, undrained

1 tablespoon red wine vinegar**DIRECTIONS**

1. Heat the oil in a large heavy pot over medium heat; cook onion and garlic until onions are translucent. Add turkey and cook, stirring, until meat is brown. Stir in beans, tomatoes, chili powder, oregano, basil and vinegar. Reduce heat to low, cover and simmer 60 minutes or more, until flavors are well blended.

BEAKER'S VEGETABLE BARLEY SOUP
Servings: 8 | Prep: 15m | Cooks: 1h30m | Total: 1h45m

NUTRITION FACTS

Calories: 188 | Carbohydrates: 37g | Fat: 1.6g | Protein: 6.9g | Cholesterol: 0mg

INGREDIENTS

- 2 quarts vegetable broth
- 1 teaspoon garlic powder
- 1 cup uncooked barley
- 1 teaspoon white sugar
- 2 large carrots, chopped
- 1 teaspoon salt
- 2 stalks celery, chopped
- 1/2 teaspoon ground black pepper
- 1 (14.5 ounce) can diced tomatoes with juice
- 1 teaspoon dried parsley
- 1 zucchini, chopped
- 1 teaspoon curry powder
- 1 (15 ounce) can garbanzo beans, drained
- 1 teaspoon paprika
- 1 onion, chopped
- 1 teaspoon Worcestershire sauce

3 bay leaves**DIRECTIONS**

1. Pour the vegetable broth into a large pot. Add the barley, carrots, celery, tomatoes, zucchini, garbanzo beans, onion, and bay leaves. Season with garlic powder, sugar, salt, pepper, parsley, curry powder, paprika, and Worcestershire sauce. Bring to a boil, then cover and simmer over medium-low heat for 90 minutes. The soup will be very thick. You may adjust by adding more broth or less barley if desired. Remove bay leaves before serving.

SLOW COOKER VEGETARIAN CHILI
Servings: 8 | Prep: 10m | Cooks: 2h | Total: 2h10m

NUTRITION FACTS

Calories: 260 | Carbohydrates: 52.6g | Fat: 2g | Protein: 12.4g | Cholesterol: 1mg

INGREDIENTS

- 1 (19 ounce) can black bean soup
- 1 green bell pepper, chopped
- 1 (15 ounce) can kidney beans, rinsed and drained
- 2 stalks celery, chopped
- 1 (15 ounce) can garbanzo beans, rinsed and drained
- 2 cloves garlic, chopped
- 1 (16 ounce) can vegetarian baked beans
- 1 tablespoon chili powder, or to taste
- 1 (14.5 ounce) can chopped tomatoes in puree
- 1 tablespoon dried parsley
- 1 (15 ounce) can whole kernel corn, drained
- 1 tablespoon dried oregano
- 1 onion, chopped

1 tablespoon dried basil**DIRECTIONS**

1. In a slow cooker, combine black bean soup, kidney beans, garbanzo beans, baked beans, tomatoes, corn, onion, bell pepper and celery. Season with garlic, chili powder, parsley, oregano and basil. Cook for at least two hours on High.

VEGAN BLACK BEAN SOUP
Servings: 6 | Prep: 15m | Cooks: 30m | Total: 45m

NUTRITION FACTS

Calories: 410 | Carbohydrates: 75.3g | Fat: 5g | Protein: 21.9g | Cholesterol: 0mg

INGREDIENTS

- 1 tablespoon olive oil
- 1 tablespoon ground cumin
- 1 large onion, chopped
- 1 pinch black pepper
- 1 stalk celery, chopped
- 4 cups vegetable broth
- 2 carrots, chopped
- 4 (15 ounce) cans black beans
- 4 cloves garlic, chopped

- 1 (15 ounce) can whole kernel corn
- 2 tablespoons chili powder

1 (14.5 ounce) can crushed tomatoes**DIRECTIONS**

1. Heat oil in a large pot over medium-high heat. Saute onion, celery, carrots and garlic for 5 minutes. Season with chili powder, cumin, and black pepper; cook for 1 minute. Stir in vegetable broth, 2 cans of beans, and corn. Bring to a boil.

2. Meanwhile, in a food processor or blender, process remaining 2 cans beans and tomatoes until smooth. Stir into boiling soup mixture, reduce heat to medium, and simmer for 15 minutes.

FIERY FISH TACOS WITH CRUNCHY CORN SALSA
Servings: 6 | Prep: 30m | Cooks: 10m | Total: 40m

NUTRITION FACTS

Calories: 351 | Carbohydrates: 40.3g | Fat: 9.6g | Protein: 28.7g | Cholesterol: 43mg

INGREDIENTS

- 2 cups cooked corn kernels
- 1 tablespoon ground black pepper
- 1/2 cup diced red onion
- 2 tablespoons salt, or to taste
- 1 cup peeled, diced jicama
- 6 (4 ounce) fillets tilapia
- 1/2 cup diced red bell pepper
- 2 tablespoons olive oil
- 1 cup fresh cilantro leaves, chopped
- 12 corn tortillas, warmed
- 1 lime, juiced and zested
- 2 tablespoons sour cream, or to taste

2 tablespoons cayenne pepper, or to taste

DIRECTIONS

1. Preheat grill for high heat.
2. In a medium bowl, mix together corn, red onion, jicama, red bell pepper, and cilantro. Stir in lime juice and zest.
3. In a small bowl, combine cayenne pepper, ground black pepper, and salt.
4. Brush each fillet with olive oil, and sprinkle with spices to taste.
5. Arrange fillets on grill grate, and cook for 3 minutes per side. For each fiery fish taco, top two corn tortillas with fish, sour cream, and corn salsa.

WHOLE WHEAT HONEY BREAD

Servings: 12 | Prep: 5m | Cooks: 3h | Total: 3h5m

NUTRITION FACTS

Calories: 148 | Carbohydrates: 30g | Fat: 2.2g | Protein: 4.6g | Cholesterol: 1mg

INGREDIENTS

- 1 1/8 cups water
- 1 tablespoon dry milk powder
- 3 cups whole wheat flour
- 1 1/2 tablespoons shortening
- 1 1/2 teaspoons salt
- 1 1/2 teaspoons active dry yeast

1/3 cup honey

DIRECTIONS

1. Place ingredients in bread machine pan in the order suggested by the manufacturer. Select Whole Wheat setting, and then press Start.

SLOW COOKER CHICKEN CACCIATORE

Servings: 6 | Prep: 15m | Cooks: 9h | Total: 9h15m

NUTRITION FACTS

Calories: 261 | Carbohydrates: 23.7g | Fat: 6.1g | Protein: 27.1g | Cholesterol: 63mg

INGREDIENTS

- 6 skinless, boneless chicken breast halves
- 8 ounces fresh mushrooms, sliced
- 1 (28 ounce) jar spaghetti sauce
- 1 onion, finely diced
- 2 green bell pepper, seeded and cubed

2 tablespoons minced garlic**DIRECTIONS**

1. Put the chicken in the slow cooker. Top with the spaghetti sauce, green bell peppers, mushrooms, onion, and garlic.
2. Cover, and cook on Low for 7 to 9 hours.

PAT'S BAKED BEANS

Servings: 10 | Prep: 15m | Cooks: 1h15m | Total: 1h30m

NUTRITION FACTS

Calories: 399 | Carbohydrates: 68g | Fat: 9.1g | Protein: 14.1g | Cholesterol: 12mg

INGREDIENTS

- 6 slices bacon
- 1 (15 ounce) can garbanzo beans, drained
- 1 cup chopped onion
- 3/4 cup ketchup
- 1 clove garlic, minced
- 1/2 cup molasses
- 1 (16 ounce) can pinto beans
- 1/4 cup packed brown sugar
- 1 (16 ounce) can great Northern beans, drained
- 2 tablespoons Worcestershire sauce
- 1 (16 ounce) can baked beans
- 1 tablespoon yellow mustard
- 1 (16 ounce) can red kidney beans, drained
- 1/2 teaspoon pepper

DIRECTIONS

1. Preheat oven to 375 degrees F (190 degrees C).
2. Place bacon in a large, deep skillet. Cook over medium high heat until evenly brown. Drain, reserving 2 tablespoons of drippings, crumble and set aside in a large bowl. Cook the onion and garlic in the reserved drippings until onion is tender; drain excess grease and transfer to the bowl with the bacon.
3. To the bacon and onions add pinto beans, northern beans, baked beans, kidney beans and garbanzo beans. Stir in ketchup, molasses, brown sugar, Worcestershire sauce, mustard and black pepper. Mix well and transfer to a 9x12 inch casserole dish.
4. Cover and bake in preheated oven for 1 hour.

BEST BLACK BEANS

Servings: 4 | Prep: 10m | Cooks: 5m | Total: 15m

NUTRITION FACTS

Calories: 112 | Carbohydrates: 20.8g | Fat: 0.4g | Protein: 7.1g | Cholesterol: 0mg

INGREDIENTS

- 1 (16 ounce) can black beans
- 1 tablespoon chopped fresh cilantro
- 1 small onion, chopped
- 1/4 teaspoon cayenne pepper
- 1 clove garlic, chopped

salt to taste**DIRECTIONS**

1. In a medium saucepan, combine beans, onion, and garlic, and bring to a boil. Reduce heat to medium-low. Season with cilantro, cayenne, and salt. Simmer for 5 minutes, and serve.

ANDREA'S PASTA FAGIOLI
Servings: 8 | Prep: 10m | Cooks: 1h30m | Total: 1h40m

NUTRITION FACTS

Calories: 403 | Carbohydrates: 68g | Fat: 7.6g | Protein: 16.3g | Cholesterol: 3mg**INGREDIENTS**

- 3 tablespoons olive oil
- 1 1/2 teaspoons dried oregano
- 1 onion, quartered then halved
- 1 teaspoon salt
- 2 cloves garlic, minced
- 1 (15 ounce) can cannellini beans
- 1 (29 ounce) can tomato sauce
- 1 (15 ounce) can navy beans
- 5 1/2 cups water
- 1/3 cup grated Parmesan cheese
- 1 tablespoon dried parsley
- 1 pound ditalini pasta

1 1/2 teaspoons dried basil

DIRECTIONS

1. In a large pot over medium heat, cook onion in olive oil until translucent. Stir in garlic and cook until tender. Reduce heat, and stir in tomato sauce, water, parsley, basil, oregano, salt, cannelini beans, navy beans and Parmesan. Simmer 1 hour.
2. Bring a large pot of lightly salted water to a boil. Add pasta and cook for 8 to 10 minutes or until al dente; drain. Stir into soup.

CHICKEN AND CORN CHILI
Servings: 6 | Prep: 15m | Cooks: 12h | Total: 12h15m

NUTRITION FACTS

Calories: 188 | Carbohydrates: 22.6g | Fat: 2.3g | Protein: 20.4g | Cholesterol: 41mg

INGREDIENTS

- 4 skinless, boneless chicken breast halves
- salt to taste
- 1 (16 ounce) jar salsa
- ground black pepper to taste
- 2 teaspoons garlic powder
- 1 (11 ounce) can Mexican-style corn
- 1 teaspoon ground cumin
- 1 (15 ounce) can pinto beans

1 teaspoon chili powder

DIRECTIONS

1. Place chicken and salsa in the slow cooker the night before you want to eat this chili. Season with garlic powder, cumin, chili powder, salt, and pepper. Cook 6 to 8 hours on Low setting.
2. About 3 to 4 hours before you want to eat, shred the chicken with 2 forks. Return the meat to the pot, and continue cooking.
3. Stir the corn and the pinto beans into the slow cooker. Simmer until ready to serve.

SLOW COOKER SPICY BLACK-EYED PEAS
Servings: 10 | Prep: 30m | Cooks: 6h | Total: 6h30m

NUTRITION FACTS

Calories: 199 | Carbohydrates: 30.2g | Fat: 2.9g | Protein: 14.1g | Cholesterol: 10mg

INGREDIENTS

- 6 cups water
- 8 ounces diced ham
- 1 cube chicken bouillon
- 4 slices bacon, chopped
- 1 pound dried black-eyed peas, sorted and rinsed
- 1/2 teaspoon cayenne pepper
- 1 onion, diced

- 1 1/2 teaspoons cumin
- 2 cloves garlic, diced
- salt, to taste
- 1 red bell pepper, stemmed, seeded, and diced
- 1 teaspoon ground black pepper

1 jalapeno chile, seeded and minced

DIRECTIONS

1. Pour the water into a slow cooker, add the bouillon cube, and stir to dissolve. Combine the black-eyed peas, onion, garlic, bell pepper, jalapeno pepper, ham, bacon, cayenne pepper, cumin, salt, and pepper; stir to blend. Cover the slow cooker and cook on Low for 6 to 8 hours until the beans are tender.

WHOLE WHEAT BLUEBERRY PANCAKES
Servings: 5 | Prep: 5m | Cooks: 8m | Total: 13m

NUTRITION FACTS

Calories: 160 | Carbohydrates: 26.7g | Fat: 2.6g | Protein: 9.8g | Cholesterol: 41mg

INGREDIENTS

- 1 1/4 cups whole wheat flour
- 1/2 teaspoon salt
- 2 teaspoons baking powder
- 1 tablespoon artificial sweetener
- 1 egg
- 1/2 cup blueberries

1 cup milk, plus more if necessary

DIRECTIONS

1. Sift together flour and baking powder, set aside. Beat together the egg, milk, salt and artificial sweetener in a bowl. Stir in flour until just moistened, add blueberries, and stir to incorporate.
2. Preheat a heavy-bottomed skillet over medium heat, and spray with cooking spray. Pour approximately 1/4 cup of the batter into the pan for each pancake. Cook until bubbly, about 1 1/2 minutes. Turn, and continue cooking until golden brown.

ROASTED BEETS 'N' SWEETS
Servings: 6 | Prep: 15m | Cooks: 1h | Total: 1h15m

NUTRITION FACTS

Calories: 195 | Carbohydrates: 33.6g | Fat: 5.9g | Protein: 3.5g | Cholesterol: 0mg

INGREDIENTS

- 6 medium beets, peeled and cut into chunks
- 1 teaspoon ground black pepper
- 2 1/2 tablespoons olive oil, divided
- 1 teaspoon sugar
- 1 teaspoon garlic powder
- 3 medium sweet potatoes, cut into chunks
- 1 teaspoon kosher salt

1 large sweet onion, chopped**DIRECTIONS**

1. Preheat oven to 400 degrees F (200 degrees C).
2. In a bowl, toss the beets with 1/2 tablespoon olive oil to coat. Spread in a single layer on a baking sheet.
3. Mix the remaining 2 tablespoons olive oil, garlic powder, salt, pepper, and sugar in a large resealable plastic bag. Place the sweet potatoes and onion in the bag. Seal bag, and shake to coat vegetables with the oil mixture.
4. Bake beets 15 minutes in the preheated oven. Mix sweet potato mixture with the beets on the baking sheet. Continue baking 45 minutes, stirring after 20 minutes, until all vegetables are tender.

FRESH TOMATO SALSA
Servings: 4 | Prep: 10m | Cooks: 1h | Total: 1h10m

NUTRITION FACTS

Calories: 51 | Carbohydrates: 9.7g | Fat: 0.2g | Protein: 2.1g | Cholesterol: 0mg

INGREDIENTS

- 3 tomatoes, chopped
- 1/2 cup chopped fresh cilantro
- 1/2 cup finely diced onion
- 1 teaspoon salt
- 5 serrano chiles, finely chopped

2 teaspoons lime juice**DIRECTIONS**

1. In a medium bowl, stir together tomatoes, onion, chili peppers, cilantro, salt, and lime juice. Chill for one hour in the refrigerator before serving.

BAKED SWEET POTATOES

Servings: 4 | Prep: 10m | Cooks: 1h5m | Total: 1h15m

NUTRITION FACTS

Calories: 321 | Carbohydrates: 61g | Fat: 7.3g | Protein: 4.8g | Cholesterol: 0mg

INGREDIENTS

- 2 tablespoons olive oil
- 2 pinches salt
- 3 large sweet potatoes
- 2 pinches ground black pepper

2 pinches dried oregano

DIRECTIONS

1. Preheat oven to 350 degrees F (175 degrees C). Coat the bottom of a glass or non-stick baking dish with olive oil, just enough to coat.
2. Wash and peel the sweet potatoes. Cut them into medium size pieces. Place the cut sweet potatoes in the baking dish and turn them so that they are coated with the olive oil. Sprinkle moderately with oregano, and salt and pepper (to taste).
3. Bake in a preheated 350 degrees F (175 degrees C) oven for 60 minutes or until soft.

CHICKPEA CURRY

Servings: 8 | Prep: 10m | Cooks: 30m | Total: 40m

NUTRITION FACTS

Calories: 135 | Carbohydrates: 20.5g | Fat: 4.5g | Protein: 4.1g | Cholesterol: 0mg

INGREDIENTS

- 2 tablespoons vegetable oil
- 1 teaspoon ground coriander
- 2 onions, minced
- salt
- 2 cloves garlic, minced
- 1 teaspoon cayenne pepper
- 2 teaspoons fresh ginger root, finely chopped
- 1 teaspoon ground turmeric
- 6 whole cloves
- 2 (15 ounce) cans garbanzo beans
- 2 (2 inch) sticks cinnamon, crushed
- 1 cup chopped fresh cilantro

1 teaspoon ground cumin

DIRECTIONS

1. Heat oil in a large frying pan over medium heat, and fry onions until tender.
2. Stir in garlic, ginger, cloves, cinnamon, cumin, coriander, salt, cayenne, and turmeric. Cook for 1 minute over medium heat, stirring constantly. Mix in garbanzo beans and their liquid. Continue to cook and stir until all ingredients are well blended and heated through. Remove from heat. Stir in cilantro just before serving, reserving 1 tablespoon for garnish.

CHICKEN FIESTA SALAD
Servings: 4 | Prep: 10m | Cooks: 30m | Total: 40m

NUTRITION FACTS

Calories: 311 | Carbohydrates: 42.2g | Fat: 6.4g | Protein: 23g | Cholesterol: 36mg

INGREDIENTS

- 2 skinless, boneless chicken breast halves
- ½ cup salsa
- 1 (1.27 ounce) packet dry fajita seasoning, divided
- 1 (10 ounce) package mixed salad greens
- 1 tablespoon vegetable oil
- 1 onion, chopped
- 1 (15 ounce) can black beans, rinsed and drained
- 1 tomato, cut into wedges

1 (11 ounce) can Mexican-style corn

DIRECTIONS

1. Rub chicken evenly with 1/2 the fajita seasoning. Heat the oil in a skillet over medium heat, and cook the chicken 8 minutes on each side, or until juices run clear; set aside.
2. In a large saucepan, mix beans, corn, salsa and other 1/2 of fajita seasoning. Heat over medium heat until warm.
3. Prepare the salad by tossing the greens, onion and tomato. Top salad with chicken and dress with the bean and corn mixture.

INSANELY EASY VEGETARIAN CHILI
Servings: 8 | Prep: 25m | Cooks: 30m | Total: 55m

NUTRITION FACTS

Calories: 155 | Carbohydrates: 29g | Fat: 3g | Protein: 6.8g | Cholesterol: 0mg

INGREDIENTS

- 1 tablespoon vegetable oil
- 1 1/2 cups chopped fresh mushrooms
- 1 cup chopped onions
- 1 (28 ounce) can whole peeled tomatoes with liquid, chopped
- 3/4 cup chopped carrots
- 1 (19 ounce) can kidney beans with liquid
- 3 cloves garlic, minced
- 1 (11 ounce) can whole kernel corn, undrained
- 1 cup chopped green bell pepper
- 1 tablespoon ground cumin
- 1 cup chopped red bell pepper
- 1 1/2 teaspoons dried oregano
- 3/4 cup chopped celery
- 1 1/2 teaspoons dried basil

1 tablespoon chili powder

DIRECTIONS

1. Heat oil in a large saucepan over medium heat. Saute onions, carrots, and garlic until tender. Stir in green pepper, red pepper, celery, and chili powder. Cook until vegetables are tender, about 6 minutes.

2. Stir in mushrooms, and cook 4 minutes. Stir in tomatoes, kidney beans, and corn. Season with cumin, oregano, and basil. Bring to a boil, and reduce heat to medium. Cover, and simmer for 20 minutes, stirring occasionally.

SPICY CHICKEN BREASTS

Servings: 4 | Prep: 15m | Cooks: 15m | Total: 30m

NUTRITION FACTS

Calories: 173 | Carbohydrates: 9.2g | Fat: 2.4g | Protein: 29.2g | Cholesterol: 68mg

INGREDIENTS

- 2 1/2 tablespoons paprika
- 1 tablespoon dried thyme
- 2 tablespoons garlic powder
- 1 tablespoon ground cayenne pepper
- 1 tablespoon salt
- 1 tablespoon ground black pepper

- 1 tablespoon onion powder

4 skinless, boneless chicken breast halves**DIRECTIONS**

1. In a medium bowl, mix together the paprika, garlic powder, salt, onion powder, thyme, cayenne pepper, and ground black pepper. Set aside about 3 tablespoons of this seasoning mixture for the chicken; store the remainder in an airtight container for later use (for seasoning fish, meats, or vegetables).
2. Preheat grill for medium-high heat. Rub some of the reserved 3 tablespoons of seasoning onto both sides of the chicken breasts.
3. Lightly oil the grill grate. Place chicken on the grill, and cook for 6 to 8 minutes on each side, until juices run clear.

BAKED BEANS
Servings: 6 | Prep: 20m | Cooks: 1h | Total: 1h20m

NUTRITION FACTS

Calories: 287 | Carbohydrates: 52.3g | Fat: 6.5g | Protein: 8.9g | Cholesterol: 16mg

INGREDIENTS

- 2 (15 ounce) cans baked beans with pork
- 1 teaspoon Worcestershire sauce
- 1/2 cup packed brown sugar
- 1 teaspoon red wine vinegar
- 1/2 onion, chopped
- salt and pepper to taste
- 1/2 cup ketchup
- 2 slices bacon

1 tablespoon prepared mustard

DIRECTIONS

1. Preheat oven to 350 degrees F (175 degrees C).
2. In a 9x9 inch baking dish, combine the pork and beans, brown sugar, onion, ketchup, mustard, Worcestershire sauce and vinegar and season with salt and pepper to taste. Top with the bacon slices.
3. Bake at 350 degrees F (175 degrees C) for 1 hour, or until sauce is thickened and bacon is cooked.

THE BEST BEAN AND HAM SOUP
Servings: 12 | Prep: 25m | Cooks: 10h | Total: 10h25m

NUTRITION FACTS

Calories: 260 | Carbohydrates: 37.9g | Fat: 3.6g | Protein: 17.3g | Cholesterol: 14mg**INGREDIENTS**

- 1 (20 ounce) package 15 bean mixture, soaked overnight
- 2 tablespoons Worcestershire sauce
- 1 ham bone
- 2 tablespoons Dijon mustard
- 2 1/2 cups cubed ham
- 1 tablespoon chili powder
- 1 large onion, chopped
- 3 bay leaves
- 3 stalks celery, chopped
- 1 teaspoon ground black pepper
- 5 large carrots, chopped
- 1 tablespoon dried parsley
- 1 (14.5 ounce) can diced tomatoes, with liquid
- 3 tablespoons lemon juice
- 1 (12 fluid ounce) can low-sodium vegetable juice
- 7 cups low fat, low sodium chicken broth
- 3 cups vegetable broth

1 teaspoon kosher salt**DIRECTIONS**

1. Place the soaked beans into a large pot and fill with enough water to cover by about 1 inch. Bring to a boil, then simmer over low for 30 minutes. Drain. Add the ham bone, ham, onion, celery, carrots, tomatoes, vegetable juice, and vegetable broth. Season with Worcestershire sauce, Dijon mustard, chili powder, bay leaves, pepper, parsley and lemon juice. Pour in enough of the chicken broth to cover the ingredients.
2. Simmer over low heat, stirring occasionally, for about 8 hours. Add more chicken broth as needed throughout the day. Remove the ham bone and season with salt if needed. Continue to simmer for a couple more hours. Remove bay leaves before serving.

VEGETARIAN KALE SOUP
Servings: 8 | Prep: 25m | Cooks: 30m | Total: 55m

NUTRITION FACTS

Calories: 277 | Carbohydrates: 50.9g | Fat: 4.5g | Protein: 9.6g | Cholesterol: 0mg**INGREDIENTS**

- 2 tablespoons olive oil
- 1 (15 ounce) can diced tomatoes
- 1 yellow onion, chopped

- 6 white potatoes, peeled and cubed
- 2 tablespoons chopped garlic
- 2 (15 ounce) cans cannellini beans (drained if desired)
- 1 bunch kale, stems removed and leaves chopped
- 1 tablespoon Italian seasoning
- 8 cups water
- 2 tablespoons dried parsley
- 6 cubes vegetable bouillon (such as Knorr)

salt and pepper to taste**DIRECTIONS**

1. Heat the olive oil in a large soup pot; cook the onion and garlic until soft. Stir in the kale and cook until wilted, about 2 minutes. Stir in the water, vegetable bouillon, tomatoes, potatoes, beans, Italian seasoning, and parsley. Simmer soup on medium heat for 25 minutes, or until potatoes are cooked through. Season with salt and pepper to taste.

HONEY ORANGE GREEN BEANS
Servings: 4 | Prep: 15m | Cooks: 25m | Total: 40m

NUTRITION FACTS

Calories: 340 | Carbohydrates: 52g | Fat: 8.9g | Protein: 14.7g | Cholesterol: 4mg

INGREDIENTS

- 1 cup vegetable broth
- 1/4 teaspoon crushed red pepper flakes
- 12 dehydrated sun-dried tomatoes
- 1 clove garlic, minced
- 1 (8 ounce) package uncooked penne pasta
- 1 bunch fresh spinach, rinsed and torn into bite-size pieces
- 2 tablespoons pine nuts
- 1/4 cup grated Parmesan cheese

1 tablespoon olive oil

DIRECTIONS

1. In a small saucepan, bring the broth to a boil. Remove from heat. Place the sun-dried tomatoes in the broth 15 minutes, or until softened. Drain, reserving broth, and coarsely chop.
2. Bring a large pot of lightly salted water to a boil. Place penne pasta in the pot, cook 9 to 12 minutes, until al dente, and drain.
3. Place the pine nuts in a skillet over medium heat. Cook and stir until lightly toasted.

4. Heat the olive oil and red pepper flakes in a skillet over medium heat, and saute the garlic 1 minute, until tender. Mix in the spinach, and cook until almost wilted. Pour in the reserved broth, and stir in the chopped sun-dried tomatoes. Continue cooking 2 minutes, or until heated through.

5. In a large bowl, toss the cooked pasta with the spinach and tomato mixture and pine nuts. Serve with Parmesan cheese.

LENTIL AND SAUSAGE SOUP
Servings: 10 | Prep: 15m | Cooks: 3h | Total: 3h15m

NUTRITION FACTS

Calories: 353 | Carbohydrates: 50.2g | Fat: 8g | Protein: 18.9g | Cholesterol: 17mg

INGREDIENTS

- 1/2 pound sweet Italian sausage
- 1 tablespoon garlic powder
- 1 large onion, chopped
- 1 tablespoon chopped fresh parsley
- 1 stalk celery, finely chopped
- 2 bay leaves
- 1 tablespoon chopped garlic
- 1/2 teaspoon dried oregano
- 1 (16 ounce) package dry lentils, rinsed
- 1/4 teaspoon dried thyme
- 1 cup shredded carrot
- 1/4 teaspoon dried basil
- 8 cups water
- 1 tablespoon salt, or to taste
- 2 (14.5 ounce) cans chicken broth
- 1/2 teaspoon black pepper
- 1 (28 ounce) can diced tomatoes

1/2 pound ditalini pasta (optional)**DIRECTIONS**

1. Place sausage in a large pot. Cook over medium high heat until evenly brown. Add onion, celery and chopped garlic, and saute until tender and translucent. Stir in lentils, carrot, water, chicken broth and tomatoes. Season with garlic powder, parsley, bay leaves, oregano, thyme, basil, salt and pepper. Bring to a boil, then reduce heat. Cover, and simmer for 2 1/2 to 3 hours, or until lentils are tender.

2. Stir in pasta, and cook 15 to 20 minutes, or until pasta is tender.

SPICY BAKED SWEET POTATO FRIES
Servings: 6 | Prep: 10m | Cooks: 1h | Total: 1h10m

NUTRITION FACTS

Calories: 169 | Carbohydrates: 29.2g | Fat: 4.7g | Protein: 2.1g | Cholesterol: 0mg

INGREDIENTS

- 6 sweet potatoes, cut into French fries
- 3 tablespoons taco seasoning mix
- 2 tablespoons canola oil

1/4 teaspoon cayenne pepper**DIRECTIONS**

1. Preheat the oven to 425 degrees F (220 degrees C).
2. In a plastic bag, combine the sweet potatoes, canola oil, taco seasoning, and cayenne pepper. Close and shake the bag until the fries are evenly coated. Spread the fries out in a single layer on two large baking sheets.
3. Bake for 30 minutes, or until crispy and brown on one side. Turn the fries over using a spatula, and cook for another 30 minutes, or until they are all crispy on the outside and tender inside. Thinner fries may not take as long.

BAKED SWEET POTATO STICKS
Servings: 8 | Prep: 15m | Cooks: 40m | Total: 55m

NUTRITION FACTS

Calories: 132 | Carbohydrates: 27g | Fat: 1.9g | Protein: 2.6g | Cholesterol: 0mg

INGREDIENTS

- 1 tablespoon olive oil
- 1/2 teaspoon paprika
- 8 sweet potatoes, sliced lengthwise into quarters

DIRECTIONS

1. Preheat oven to 400 degrees F (200 degrees C). Lightly grease a baking sheet.
2. In a large bowl, mix olive oil and paprika. Add potato sticks, and stir by hand to coat. Place on the prepared baking sheet.
3. Bake 40 minutes in the preheated oven.

WHOLE WHEAT AND HONEY PIZZA DOUGH
Servings: 12 | Prep: 10m | Cooks: 10m | Total: 20m

NUTRITION FACTS

Calories: 83 | Carbohydrates: 17.4g | Fat: 0.6g | Protein: 3.5g | Cholesterol: 0mg

INGREDIENTS

- 1 (.25 ounce) package active dry yeast
- 1/4 cup wheat germ
- 1 cup warm water
- 1 teaspoon salt
- 2 cups whole wheat flour

1 tablespoon honey**DIRECTIONS**

1. Preheat oven to 350 degrees F (175 degrees C).
2. In a small bowl, dissolve yeast in warm water. Let stand until creamy, about 10 minutes.
3. In a large bowl combine flour, wheat germ and salt. Make a well in the middle and add honey and yeast mixture. Stir well to combine. Cover and set in a warm place to rise for a few minutes.
4. Roll dough on a floured pizza pan and poke a few holes in it with a fork.
5. Bake in preheated oven for 5 to 10 minutes, or until desired crispiness is achieved.

GREEK PASTA WITH TOMATOES AND WHITE BEANS

Servings: 4 | Prep: 10m | Cooks: 15m | Total: 25m

NUTRITION FACTS

Calories: 460 | Carbohydrates: 79g | Fat: 5.9g | Protein: 23.4g | Cholesterol: 17mg

INGREDIENTS

- 2 (14.5 ounce) cans Italian-style diced tomatoes
- 8 ounces penne pasta
- 1 (19 ounce) can cannellini beans, drained and rinsed
- 1/2 cup crumbled feta cheese

10 ounces fresh spinach, washed and chopped

DIRECTIONS

1. Cook the pasta in a large pot of boiling salted water until al dente.
2. Meanwhile, combine tomatoes and beans in a large non-stick skillet. Bring to a boil over medium high heat. Reduce heat, and simmer 10 minutes.
3. Add spinach to the sauce; cook for 2 minutes or until spinach wilts, stirring constantly.
4. Serve sauce over pasta, and sprinkle with feta.

SLOW COOKER CHICKEN MARRAKESH

Servings: 8 | Prep: 25m | Cooks: 4h | Total: 4h25m

NUTRITION FACTS

Calories: 290 | Carbohydrates: 36g | Fat: 2g | Protein: 30.6g | Cholesterol: 66mg

INGREDIENTS

- 1 onion, sliced
- 1/2 teaspoon ground turmeric
- 2 cloves garlic, minced (optional)
- ¼ teaspoon ground cinnamon
- 2 large carrots, peeled and diced
- 1/2 teaspoon ground black pepper
- 2 large sweet potatoes, peeled and diced
- 1 teaspoon dried parsley
- 1 (15 ounce) can garbanzo beans, drained and rinsed
- 1 teaspoon salt
- 2 pounds skinless, boneless chicken breast halves, cut into 2-inch pieces
- 1 (14.5 ounce) can diced tomatoes

1/2 teaspoon ground cumin

DIRECTIONS

1. Place the onion, garlic, carrots, sweet potatoes, garbanzo beans, and chicken breast pieces into a slow cooker. In a bowl, mix the cumin, turmeric, cinnamon, black pepper, parsley, and salt, and sprinkle over the chicken and vegetables. Pour in the tomatoes, and stir to combine.
2. Cover the cooker, set to High, and cook until the sweet potatoes are tender and the sauce has thickened, 4 to 5 hours.

MIDDLE EASTERN RICE WITH BLACK BEANS AND CHICKPEAS

Servings: 8 | Prep: 15m | Cooks: 45m | Total: 1h

NUTRITION FACTS

Calories: 452 | Carbohydrates: 55.7g | Fat: 12.2g | Protein: 30.7g | Cholesterol: 65mg

INGREDIENTS

- 1 tablespoon olive oil
- 1 1/2 pounds ground turkey

- 1 clove garlic, minced
- 2 (15 ounce) cans garbanzo beans (chickpeas), drained and rinsed
- 1 cup uncooked basmati rice
- 2 (15 ounce) cans black beans, drained and rinsed
- 2 teaspoons ground cumin
- 1 bunch chopped fresh cilantro (optional)
- 2 teaspoons ground coriander
- 1 bunch chopped fresh parsley (optional)
- 1 teaspoon ground turmeric
- 1/4 cup pine nuts (optional)
- 1 teaspoon ground cayenne pepper
- salt and ground black pepper to taste

1 quart chicken stock

DIRECTIONS

1. Heat the olive oil in a large saucepan over medium heat. Stir in garlic, and cook 1 minute. Stir in rice, cumin, coriander, turmeric, and cayenne pepper. Cook and stir 5 minutes, then pour in chicken stock. Bring to a boil. Reduce heat to low, cover, and simmer 20 minutes.
2. Place the turkey in a skillet over medium heat, and cook until evenly brown.
3. Gently mix cooked turkey, garbanzo beans, black beans, cilantro, parsley, and pine nuts into the cooked rice. Season with salt and pepper.

MOROCCAN LENTIL SOUP
Servings: 6 | Prep: 20m | Cooks: 1h45m | Total: 2h5m

NUTRITION FACTS

Calories: 329 | Carbohydrates: 56.5g | Fat: 3.6g | Protein: 18.3g | Cholesterol: 0mg**INGREDIENTS**

- 2 onions, chopped
- 1/2 cup diced carrots
- 2 cloves garlic, minced
- 1/2 cup chopped celery
- 1 teaspoon grated fresh ginger
- 1 teaspoon garam masala
- 6 cups water
- 1 1/2 teaspoons ground cardamom
- 1 cup red lentils
- 1/2 teaspoon ground cayenne pepper
- 1 (15 ounce) can garbanzo beans, drained
- 1/2 teaspoon ground cumin
- 1 (19 ounce) can cannellini beans

- 1 tablespoon olive oil

1 (14.5 ounce) can diced tomatoes

DIRECTIONS

1. In large pot saute; the onions, garlic, and ginger in a little olive oil for about 5 minutes.
2. Add the water, lentils, chick peas, white kidney beans, diced tomatoes, carrots, celery, garam masala, cardamom, cayenne pepper and cumin. Bring to a boil for a few minutes then simmer for 1 to 1 1/2 hours or longer, until the lentils are soft.
3. Puree half the soup in a food processor or blender. Return the pureed soup to the pot, stir and enjoy!

BLACK-EYED PEA GUMBO

Servings: 8 | Prep: 15m | Cooks: 55m | Total: 1h10m

NUTRITION FACTS

Calories: 272 | Carbohydrates: 48.5g | Fat: 3.4g | Protein: 12.5g | Cholesterol: 0mg

INGREDIENTS

- 1 tablespoon olive oil
- 1 cup brown rice
- 1 medium onion, chopped
- 4 (15 ounce) cans black-eyed peas with liquid
- 1 medium green bell pepper, chopped
- 1 (10 ounce) can diced tomatoes and green chiles
- 5 stalks celery, chopped
- 1 (14.5 ounce) can diced tomatoes
- 2 cups chicken broth

2 cloves garlic, finely chopped**DIRECTIONS**

1. Heat the olive oil in a large saucepan over medium heat, and cook the onion, pepper, and celery until tender. Pour in the chicken broth, and mix in rice, black-eyed peas with liquid, diced tomatoes and green chiles, diced tomatoes, and garlic. Bring to a boil, reduce heat to low, and simmer 45 minutes, or until rice is tender. Add water if soup is too thick.

EASY RED BEANS AND RICE

Servings: 8 | Prep: 10m | Cooks: 30m | Total: 40m

NUTRITION FACTS

Calories: 289 | Carbohydrates: 42.4g | Fat: 5.7g | Protein: 16.3g | Cholesterol: 35mg

INGREDIENTS

- 2 cups water
- 2 (15 ounce) cans canned kidney beans, drained
- 1 cup uncooked rice
- 1 (16 ounce) can whole peeled tomatoes, chopped
- 1 (16 ounce) package turkey kielbasa, cut diagonally into 1/4 inch slices
- 1/2 teaspoon dried oregano
- 1 onion, chopped
- salt to taste
- 1 green bell pepper, chopped
- 1/2 teaspoon pepper
- 1 clove chopped garlic

DIRECTIONS

1. In a saucepan, bring water to a boil. Add rice and stir. Reduce heat, cover and simmer for 20 minutes.
2. In a large skillet over low heat, cook sausage for 5 minutes. Stir in onion, green pepper and garlic; saute until tender. Pour in beans and tomatoes with juice. Season with oregano, salt and pepper. Simmer uncovered for 20 minutes. Serve over rice.

CRANBERRY AND CILANTRO QUINOA SALAD
Servings: 6 | Prep: 10m | Cooks: 20m | Total: 2h30m

NUTRITION FACTS

Calories: 176 | Carbohydrates: 31.6g | Fat: 3..9g | Protein: 5.4g | Cholesterol: 0mg

INGREDIENTS

- 1 1/2 cups water
- 1/4 cup chopped fresh cilantro
- 1 cup uncooked quinoa, rinsed
- 1 lime, juiced
- 1/4 cup red bell pepper, chopped
- 1/4 cup toasted sliced almonds
- 1/4 cup yellow bell pepper, chopped
- 1/2 cup minced carrots
- 1 small red onion, finely chopped
- 1/2 cup dried cranberries
- 1 1/2 teaspoons curry powder
- salt and ground black pepper to taste

DIRECTIONS

1. Pour the water into a saucepan, and cover with a lid. Bring to a boil over high heat, then pour in the quinoa, recover, and continue to simmer over low heat until the water has been absorbed, 15 to 20 minutes. Scrape into a mixing bowl, and chill in the refrigerator until cold.

2. Once cold, stir in the red bell pepper, yellow bell pepper, red onion, curry powder, cilantro, lime juice, sliced almonds, carrots, and cranberries. Season to taste with salt and pepper. Chill before serving.

SPICY SLOW COOKER BLACK BEAN SOUP
Servings: 6 | Prep: 5m | Cooks: 6h| Total: 6h5m

NUTRITION FACTS

Calories: 281 | Carbohydrates: 49.7g | Fat: 2g | Protein: 17.7g | Cholesterol: 5mg

INGREDIENTS

- 1 pound dry black beans, soaked overnight
- 1 teaspoon ground cumin
- 4 teaspoons diced jalapeno peppers
- 1 teaspoon cayenne pepper
- 6 cups chicken broth
- 3/4 teaspoon ground black pepper
- 1/2 teaspoon garlic powder
- 1/2 teaspoon hot pepper sauce

1 tablespoon chili powder

DIRECTIONS

1. Drain black beans, and rinse.
2. Combine beans, jalapenos, and chicken broth in a slow cooker. Season with garlic powder, chili powder, cumin, cayenne, pepper, and hot pepper sauce.
3. Cook on High for 4 hours. Reduce heat to Low, and continue cooking for 2 hours, or until you are ready to eat.

PASTA FAGIOLI
Servings: 4 | Prep: 10m | Cooks: 40m | Total: 40m

NUTRITION FACTS

Calories: 225 | Carbohydrates: 37.3g | Fat: 4.4g | Protein: 11g | Cholesterol: 2mg

INGREDIENTS

- 1 tablespoon olive oil
- salt to taste
- 2 stalks celery, chopped
- 1 (14.5 ounce) can chicken broth
- 1 onion, chopped
- 2 medium tomatoes, peeled and chopped
- 3 cloves garlic, minced
- 1 (8 ounce) can tomato sauce
- 2 teaspoons dried parsley
- 1/2 cup uncooked spinach pasta
- 1 teaspoon Italian seasoning
- 1 (15 ounce) can cannellini beans, with liquid
- 1/4 teaspoon crushed red pepper flakes

DIRECTIONS

1. Heat olive oil in a large saucepan over medium heat. Cook celery, onion, garlic, parsley, Italian seasoning, red pepper flakes, and salt in the hot oil until onion is translucent, about 5 minutes. Stir in chicken broth, tomatoes and tomato sauce, and simmer on low for 15 to 20 minutes.
2. Add pasta and cook 10 minutes, until pasta is tender.
3. Add undrained beans and mix well. Heat through. Serve with grated Parmesan cheese sprinkled on top.

JERRE'S BLACK BEAN AND PORK TENDERLOIN SLOW COOKER CHILI

Servings: 8 | Prep: 10m | Cooks: 10h | Total: 10h10m

NUTRITION FACTS

Calories: 245 | Carbohydrates: 31.9g | Fat: 2.8g | Protein: 24g | Cholesterol: 37mg

INGREDIENTS

- 1 1/2 pounds pork tenderloin, cut into 2 inch strips
- 1/2 cup chicken broth
- 1 small onion, coarsely chopped
- 1 teaspoon dried oregano
- 1 small red bell pepper, coarsely chopped
- 1 teaspoon ground cumin
- 3 (15 ounce) cans black beans
- 2 teaspoons chili powder
- 1 (16 ounce) jar salsa

DIRECTIONS

1. Combine pork tenderloin, onion, red pepper, black beans, salsa, chicken broth, oregano, cumin, and chili powder in a slow cooker. Set to Low and cook for 8 to 10 hours.
2. Break up pieces of cooked pork to thicken the chili before serving.

MIMI'S GIANT WHOLE-WHEAT BANANA-STRAWBERRY MUFFINS

Servings: 12 | Prep: 15m | Cooks: 20m | Total: 35m

NUTRITION FACTS

Calories: 212 | Carbohydrates: 38.1g | Fat: 5.9g | Protein: 4.2g | Cholesterol: 31mg

INGREDIENTS

- 2 eggs
- 3 bananas, mashed
- 1/2 cup unsweetened applesauce
- 2 cups whole wheat flour
- 1/4 cup vegetable oil
- 1 teaspoon baking soda
- 3/4 cup packed brown sugar
- 1 tablespoon ground cinnamon
- 1 teaspoon vanilla extract
- 1 cup frozen sliced strawberries

DIRECTIONS

1. Preheat the oven to 375 degrees F (190 degrees C). Grease 12 large muffin cups, or line with paper liners.
2. In a large bowl, whisk together the eggs, applesauce, oil, brown sugar, vanilla and bananas. Combine the flour, baking soda and cinnamon; Stir into the banana mixture until moistened. Stir in the strawberries until evenly distributed. Spoon batter into muffin cups until completely filled.
3. Bake for 20 minutes in the preheated oven, or until the tops of the muffins spring back when pressed lightly. Cool before removing from the muffin tins.

BAKED TORTILLA CHIPS

Servings: 6 | Prep: 10m | Cooks: 15m | Total: 25m

NUTRITION FACTS

Calories: 147 | Carbohydrates: 26g | Fat: 4.1 g | Protein: 3.3g | Cholesterol: 0mg

INGREDIENTS

- 1 (12 ounce) package corn tortillas
- 1 teaspoon ground cumin
- 1 tablespoon vegetable oil
- 1 teaspoon chili powder
- 3 tablespoons lime juice
- 1 teaspoon salt

DIRECTIONS

1. Preheat oven to 350 degrees F (175 degrees C).
2. Cut each tortilla into 8 chip sized wedges and arrange the wedges in a single layer on a cookie sheet.
3. In a mister, combine the oil and lime juice. Mix well and spray each tortilla wedge until slightly moist.
4. Combine the cumin, chili powder and salt in a small bowl and sprinkle on the chips.
5. Bake for about 7 minutes. Rotate the pan and bake for another 8 minutes or until the chips are crisp, but not too brown. Serve with salsas, garnishes or guacamole.

PERFECT SUMMER FRUIT SALAD
Servings: 10 | Prep: 25m | Cooks: 5m | Total: 3h30m

NUTRITION FACTS

Calories: 155 | Carbohydrates: 39g | Fat: 0.6g | Protein: 1.8g | Cholesterol: 0mg

INGREDIENTS

- 2/3 cup fresh orange juice
- 2 cups strawberries, hulled and sliced
- 1/3 cup fresh lemon juice
- 3 kiwi fruit, peeled and sliced
- 1/3 cup packed brown sugar
- 3 bananas, sliced
- 1/2 teaspoon grated orange zest
- 2 oranges, peeled and sectioned
- 1/2 teaspoon grated lemon zest
- 1 cup seedless grapes
- 1 teaspoon vanilla extract
- 2 cups blueberries
- 2 cups cubed fresh pineapple

DIRECTIONS

1. Bring orange juice, lemon juice, brown sugar, orange zest, and lemon zest to a boil in a saucepan over medium-high heat. Reduce heat to medium-low, and simmer until slightly thickened, about 5 minutes. Remove from heat, and stir in vanilla extract. Set aside to cool.

2. Layer the fruit in a large, clear glass bowl in this order: pineapple, strawberries, kiwi fruit, bananas, oranges, grapes, and blueberries. Pour the cooled sauce over the fruit. Cover and refrigerate for 3 to 4 hours before serving.

SPLIT PEA AND HAM SOUP

Servings: 4 | Prep: 5m | Cooks: 2h5m | Total: 2h30m | Additional: 20m

NUTRITION FACTS

Calories: 413 | Carbohydrates: 72.2g | Fat: 2.5g | Protein: 28.3g | Cholesterol: 0mg

INGREDIENTS

- 1 cup chopped onion
- 1 pound ham bone
- 1 teaspoon vegetable oil
- 1 pinch salt and pepper to taste
- 1 pound dried split peas

DIRECTIONS

1. In a medium pot, saute onions in oil. Add the split peas, ham bone, and enough water to cover ingredients; season with salt and pepper.
2. Cover, and cook until there are no peas left, just a green liquid, 2 hours. While it is cooking, check to see if water has evaporated. You may need to add more water as the soup continues to cook.
3. Once the soup is a green liquid remove from heat, and let stand so it will thicken. Once thickened you may need to heat through to serve.

BLACKENED TILAPIA WITH SECRET HOBO SPICES

Servings: 4 | Prep: 10m | Cooks: 8m | Total: 18m

NUTRITION FACTS

Calories: 245 | Carbohydrates: 21.5g | Fat: 6.8g | Protein: 26.8g | Cholesterol: 42mg

INGREDIENTS

- 3 tablespoons paprika
- 1 teaspoon dried thyme
- 1 tablespoon onion powder
- 1/2 teaspoon celery seed
- 1 pinch garlic powder
- 1 tablespoon kosher salt, or to taste

- 1 teaspoon ground white pepper
- 1 pound tilapia fillets
- 1 teaspoon ground black pepper
- 1 lemon, cut into wedges
- 1 teaspoon cayenne pepper, or to taste
- 4 slices white bread
- 1 teaspoon dried oregano
- 1 tablespoon vegetable oil

DIRECTIONS

1. In a small bowl or jar with a lid, make the spice blend. Mix together the paprika, onion powder, garlic powder, white pepper, black pepper, cayenne pepper, oregano, thyme, celery seed and kosher salt. Coat the fish fillets with the spice mixture, and allow to sit at room temperature for no longer than 30 minutes.

2. Heat a heavy skillet over high heat. Add oil, and heat until it is almost smoking. Place the fillets in the pan, and cook for about 3 minutes per side, or until fish is opaque and can be flaked with a fork. Remove from the pan, and place onto slices of white bread. Pour pan juices over them and squeeze lemon juice all over. Do not underestimate the white bread. It gets quite tasty soaking up all the juices.

HAM BONE SOUP

Servings: 4 | Prep: 30m | Cooks: 6h | Total: 6h30m

NUTRITION FACTS

Calories: 266 | Carbohydrates: 53.3g | Fat: 1g | Protein: 11.4g | Cholesterol: 1mg

INGREDIENTS

- 1 ham bone with some meat
- 3 potatoes, cubed
- 1 onion, diced
- 1 green bell pepper, seeded and cubed
- 1 (14.5 ounce) can peeled and diced tomatoes with juice
- 4 cups water
- 1 (15.25 ounce) can kidney beans

6 cubes chicken bouillon**DIRECTIONS**

1. Place the ham bone, onion, tomatoes, kidney beans, potatoes, and green pepper into a 3 quart or larger slow cooker. Dissolve the bouillon cubes in water, and pour into the slow cooker.

2. Cover, and cook on High until warm. Reduce heat to Low, and continue to cook for 5 to 6 hours.

SPINACH AND LEEK WHITE BEAN SOUP

Servings: 8 | Prep: 10m | Cooks: 15m | Total: 25m

NUTRITION FACTS

Calories: 179 | Carbohydrates: 30.6g | Fat: 2g | Protein: 9.4g | Cholesterol: 0mg

INGREDIENTS

- 2 teaspoons olive oil
- 2 bay leaves
- 4 leeks, bulb only, chopped
- 2 teaspoons ground cumin
- 2 cloves garlic, chopped
- 1/2 cup whole wheat couscous
- 2 (16 ounce) cans fat-free chicken broth
- 2 cups packed fresh spinach
- 2 (16 ounce) cans cannellini beans, rinsed and drained

salt and pepper to taste**DIRECTIONS**

1. Heat olive oil in a large saucepan or soup pot over medium heat. Add the leeks and garlic; saute until tender, about 5 minutes. Stir in the chicken broth, cannellini beans, bay leaves and cumin. Bring to a boil, then reduce the heat to low, and stir in the couscous. Cover, and simmer for 5 minutes. Stir in spinach and season with salt and pepper. Serve immediately.

QUINOA AND BLACK BEAN CHILI

Servings: 10 | Prep: 30m | Cooks: 30m | Total: 1h

NUTRITION FACTS

Calories: 233 | Carbohydrates: 42g | Fat: 3.5g | Protein: 11.5g | Cholesterol: 0mg

INGREDIENTS

- 1 cup uncooked quinoa, rinsed
- 1 green bell pepper, chopped
- 2 cups water
- 1 red bell pepper, chopped
- 1 tablespoon vegetable oil
- 1 zucchini, chopped
- 1 onion, chopped
- 1 jalapeno pepper, seeded and minced
- 4 cloves garlic, chopped

- 1 tablespoon minced chipotle peppers in adobo sauce
- 1 tablespoon chili powder
- 1 teaspoon dried oregano
- 1 tablespoon ground cumin
- salt and ground black pepper to taste
- 1 (28 ounce) can crushed tomatoes
- 1 cup frozen corn
- 2 (19 ounce) cans black beans, rinsed and drained
- 1/4 cup chopped fresh cilantro

DIRECTIONS

1. Bring the quinoa and water to a boil in a saucepan over high heat. Reduce heat to medium-low, cover, and simmer until the quinoa is tender, and the water has been absorbed, about 15 to 20 minutes; set aside.
2. Meanwhile, heat the vegetable oil in a large pot over medium heat. Stir in the onion, and cook until the onion softens and turns translucent, about 5 minutes. Add the garlic, chili powder, and cumin; cook and stir 1 minute to release the flavors. Stir in the tomatoes, black beans, green bell pepper, red bell pepper, zucchini, jalapeno pepper, chipotle pepper, and oregano. Season to taste with salt and pepper. Bring to a simmer over high heat, then reduce heat to medium-low, cover, and simmer 20 minutes.
3. After 20 minutes, stir in the reserved quinoa and corn. Cook to reheat the corn for 5 minutes.

   Remove from the heat, and stir in the cilantro to serve.

MOROCCAN-STYLE STUFFED ACORN SQUASH
Servings: 4 | Prep: 15m | Cooks: 45m | Total: 1h

NUTRITION FACTS

Calories: 502 | Carbohydrates: 93.8g | Fat: 11.7g | Protein: 11.2g | Cholesterol: 10mg

INGREDIENTS

- 2 tablespoons brown sugar
- 1 cup garbanzo beans, drained
- 1 tablespoon butter, melted
- 1/2 cup raisins
- 2 large acorn squash, halved and seeded
- 1 1/2 tablespoons ground cumin
- 2 tablespoons olive oil
- salt and pepper to taste
- 2 cloves garlic, chopped
- 1 (14 ounce) can chicken broth
- 2 stalks celery, chopped
- 1 cup uncooked couscous

2 carrots, chopped

DIRECTIONS

1. Preheat oven to 350 degrees F (175 degrees C).
2. Arrange squash halves cut side down on a baking sheet. Bake 30 minutes, or until tender. Dissolve the sugar in the melted butter. Brush squash with the butter mixture, and keep squash warm while preparing the stuffing.
3. Heat the olive oil in a skillet over medium heat. Stir in the garlic, celery, and carrots, and cook 5 minutes. Mix in the garbanzo beans and raisins. Season with cumin, salt, and pepper, and continue to cook and stir until vegetables are tender.
4. Pour the chicken broth into the skillet, and mix in the couscous. Cover skillet, and turn off heat.

   Allow couscous to absorb liquid for 5 minutes. Stuff squash halves with the skillet mixture to serve.

HAM AND BEANS
Servings: 7 | Prep: 15m | Cooks: 2h | Total: 10h15m | Additional: 8h

NUTRITION FACTS

Calories: 300 | Carbohydrates: 42.8g | Fat: 6.7g | Protein: 18.6g | Cholesterol: 18mg

INGREDIENTS

- 1 pound dry great Northern beans
- salt and pepper to taste
- 1/2 pound cooked ham, diced
- 1/4 teaspoon cayenne pepper
- 1 small onion, diced
- 1 tablespoon dried parsley

1/2 cup brown sugar

DIRECTIONS

1. Rinse beans in a large pot; discard shriveled beans and any small stones. Add 8 cups of cold water. Let stand overnight or at least 8 hours. Drain and rinse beans.
2. Return beans to pot and add ham, onion, brown sugar, salt, pepper, cayenne and parsley and water to cover. Bring to a boil; reduce heat and simmer 1 1/2 to 2 hours, until beans are tender. Add more water if necessary during cooking time.

MICROWAVE POPCORN
Servings: 3 | Prep: 2m | Cooks: 3m | Total: 5m

NUTRITION FACTS

Calories: 137 | Carbohydrates: 24.6g | Fat: 3.1g | Protein: 4.1g | Cholesterol: 0mg

INGREDIENTS

- 1/2 cup unpopped popcorn
- 1/2 teaspoon salt, or to taste

1 teaspoon vegetable oil

DIRECTIONS

1. In a cup or small bowl, mix together the unpopped popcorn and oil. Pour the coated corn into a brown paper lunch sack, and sprinkle in the salt. Fold the top of the bag over twice to seal in the ingredients.
2. Cook in the microwave at full power for 2 1/2 to 3 minutes, or until you hear pauses of about 2 seconds between pops. Carefully open the bag to avoid steam, and pour into a serving bowl.

BUTTERNUT SQUASH AND TURKEY CHILI
Servings: 12 | Prep: 20m | Cooks: 30m | Total: 50m

NUTRITION FACTS

Calories: 165 | Carbohydrates: 20.5g | Fat: 3.3g | Protein: 13.4g | Cholesterol: 24mg

INGREDIENTS

- 2 tablespoons olive oil
- 2 (14.5 ounce) cans petite diced tomatoes
- 1 onion, chopped
- 1 (15 ounce) can kidney beans with liquid
- 2 cloves garlic, minced
- 1 (15.5 ounce) can white hominy, drained
- 1 pound ground turkey breast
- 1 (8 ounce) can tomato sauce
- 1 pound butternut squash - peeled, seeded and cut into 1-inch dice
- 1 tablespoon chili powder
- 1/2 cup chicken broth
- 1 tablespoon ground cumin
- 1 (4.5 ounce) can chopped green chilies

1 teaspoon garlic salt**DIRECTIONS**

1. Heat the olive oil in a large pot over medium heat. Stir in the onion and garlic; cook and stir for 3 minutes, then add the turkey, and stir until crumbly and no longer pink.

2. Add the butternut squash, chicken broth, green chilies, tomatoes, kidney beans, hominy, and tomato sauce; season with chili powder, cumin, and garlic salt. Bring to a simmer, then reduce heat to medium-low, cover, and simmer until the squash is tender, about 20 minutes.

QUICK AND EASY PANCIT
Servings: 6 | Prep: 20m | Cooks: 20m | Total: 40m

NUTRITION FACTS

Calories: 369 | Carbohydrates: 65.1g | Fat: 4.9g | Protein: 18.1g | Cholesterol: 35mg

INGREDIENTS

- 1 (12 ounce) package dried rice noodles
- 1 small head cabbage, thinly sliced
- 1 teaspoon vegetable oil
- 4 carrot, thinly sliced
- 1 onion, finely diced
- 1/4 cup soy sauce
- 3 cloves garlic, minced
- 2 lemons - cut into wedges, for garnish

2 cups diced cooked chicken breast meat

DIRECTIONS

1. Place the rice noodles in a large bowl, and cover with warm water. When soft, drain, and set aside.
2. Heat oil in a wok or large skillet over medium heat. Saute onion and garlic until soft. Stir in chicken cabbage, carrots and soy sauce. Cook until cabbage begins to soften. Toss in noodles, and cook until heated through, stirring constantly. Transfer pancit to a serving dish and garnish with quartered lemons.

STOVETOP MOROCCAN TAGINE
Servings: 6 | Prep: 15m | Cooks: 45m | Total: 1h

NUTRITION FACTS

Calories: 265 | Carbohydrates: 44.7g | Fat: 4.3g | Protein: 14.1g | Cholesterol: 20mg

INGREDIENTS

- 1 tablespoon olive oil
- 1 (14.5 ounce) can diced tomatoes with juice

- 2 skinless, boneless chicken breast halves - cut into chunks
- 1 (14 ounce) can vegetable broth
- ½ onion, chopped
- 1 tablespoon sugar
- 3 cloves garlic, minced
- 1 tablespoon lemon juice
- 1 small butternut squash, peeled and chopped
- 1 teaspoon salt
- 1 (15.5 ounce) can garbanzo beans, drained and rinsed
- 1 teaspoon ground coriander
- 1 carrot, peeled and chopped

1 dash cayenne pepper **DIRECTIONS**

1. Heat the olive oil in a large skillet over medium heat, and cook the chicken, onion, and garlic about 15 minutes, until browned.
2. Mix the squash, garbanzo beans, carrot, tomatoes with juice, broth, sugar, and lemon juice into the skillet. Season with salt, coriander, and cayenne pepper. Bring the mixture to a boil, and continue cooking 30 minutes, until vegetables are tender.

VEGAN SPLIT PEA SOUP
Servings: 10 | Prep: 10m | Cooks: 3h | Total: 3h10m

NUTRITION FACTS

Calories: 247 | Carbohydrates: 45.8g | Fat: 1.3g | Protein: 12.7g | Cholesterol: 0mg

INGREDIENTS

- 1 tablespoon vegetable oil
- 3 carrots, chopped
- 1 onion, chopped
- 3 stalks celery, chopped
- 1 bay leaf
- 3 potatoes, diced
- 3 cloves garlic, minced
- 1/2 cup chopped parsley
- 2 cups dried split peas
- 1/2 teaspoon dried basil
- 1/2 cup barley
- 1/2 teaspoon dried thyme
- 1 1/2 teaspoons salt
- 1/2 teaspoon ground black pepper

7 1/2 cups water

DIRECTIONS

1. In a large pot over medium high heat, saute the oil, onion, bay leaf and garlic for 5 minutes, or until onions are translucent. Add the peas, barley, salt and water. Bring to a boil and reduce heat to low. Simmer for 2 hours, stirring occasionally.

2. Add the carrots, celery, potatoes, parsley, basil, thyme and ground black pepper. Simmer for another hour, or until the peas and vegetables are tender.

NAVY BEAN SOUP
Servings: 9 | Prep: 15m | Cooks: 4h10m | Total: 4h25m

NUTRITION FACTS

Calories: 236 | Carbohydrates: 35.7g | Fat: 3.4g | Protein: 16.1g | Cholesterol: 15mg

INGREDIENTS

- 1 (16 ounce) package dried navy beans
- 2 tablespoons Worcestershire sauce
- 6 cups water
- 1 tablespoon dried parsley
- 1 (14.5 ounce) can diced tomatoes
- 2 teaspoons garlic powder
- 1 onion, chopped
- 1 bay leaf
- 2 stalks celery, chopped
- 1 teaspoon salt
- 1 clove garlic, minced
- 1/2 teaspoon ground black pepper
- 1/2 pound chopped ham
- 3 cups water

1 cube chicken bouillon

DIRECTIONS

1. Combine beans, water, tomatoes, onion, celery, garlic, ham, bouillon, Worcestershire sauce, parsley, garlic, and bay leaf in a stock pot; bring to a boil. Lower heat, cover, and simmer for two hours.
2. Add additional water. Season with salt and pepper. Simmer for an additional two hours. Discard bay leaf.

LENTILS AND SPINACH

Servings: 4 | Prep: 10m | Cooks: 55m | Total: 1h5m

NUTRITION FACTS

Calories: 165 | Carbohydrates: 24g | Fat: 4.3g | Protein: 9.7g | Cholesterol: 0mg

INGREDIENTS

- 1 tablespoon vegetable oil
- 1 (10 ounce) package frozen spinach
- 2 white onions, halved and sliced into 1/2 rings
- 1 teaspoon salt
- 3 cloves garlic, minced
- 1 teaspoon ground cumin
- 1/2 cup lentils
- freshly ground black pepper to taste
- 2 cups water

2 cloves garlic, crushed**DIRECTIONS**

1. Heat oil in a heavy pan over medium heat. Saute onion for 10 minutes or so, until it begins to turn golden. Add minced garlic and saute for another minute or so.
2. Add lentils and water to the saucepan. Bring mixture to a boil. Cover, lower heat, and simmer about 35 minutes, until lentils are soft (this may take less time, depending on your water and the lentils).
3. Meanwhile cook the spinach in microwave according to package directions. Add spinach, salt and cumin to the saucepan. Cover and simmer until all is heated, about ten minutes. Grind in plenty of pepper and press in extra garlic to taste.

TERRY'S TEXAS PINTO BEANS

Servings: 8 | Prep: 15m | Cooks: 2h | Total: 2h15m

NUTRITION FACTS

Calories: 210 | Carbohydrates: 37.9g | Fat: 1.1g | Protein: 13.2g | Cholesterol: 1mg

INGREDIENTS

- 1 pound dry pinto beans
- 1/2 cup green salsa
- 1 (29 ounce) can reduced sodium chicken broth
- 1 teaspoon cumin
- 1 large onion, chopped
- 1/2 teaspoon ground black pepper
- 1 fresh jalapeno pepper, chopped

- water, if needed

2 cloves garlic, minced

DIRECTIONS

1. Place the pinto beans in a large pot, and pour in the chicken broth. Stir in onion, jalapeno, garlic, salsa, cumin, and pepper. Bring to a boil, reduce heat to medium-low, and continue cooking 2 hours, stirring often, until beans are tender. Add water as needed to keep the beans moist.

ESPINACAS CON GARBANZOS (SPINACH WITH GARBANZO BEANS)
Servings: 4 | Prep: 15m | Cooks: 10m | Total: 25m

NUTRITION FACTS

Calories: 169 | Carbohydrates: 26g | Fat: 4.9g | Protein: 7.3g | Cholesterol: 0mg

INGREDIENTS

- 1 tablespoon extra-virgin olive oil
- 1 (12 ounce) can garbanzo beans, drained
- 4 cloves garlic, minced
- 1/2 teaspoon cumin
- 1/2 onion, diced
- 1/2 teaspoon salt

1 (10 ounce) box frozen chopped spinach, thawed and drained well

DIRECTIONS

1. Heat the olive oil in a skillet over medium-low heat. Cook the garlic and onion in the oil until translucent, about 5 minutes. Stir in the spinach, garbanzo beans, cumin, and salt. Use your stirring spoon to lightly mash the beans as the mixture cooks. Allow to cook until thoroughly heated.

VEGAN BEAN TACO FILLING
Servings: 8 | Prep: 15m | Cooks: 15m | Total: 30m

NUTRITION FACTS

Calories: 142 | Carbohydrates: 24g | Fat: 2.5g | Protein: 7.5g | Cholesterol: 0mg

INGREDIENTS

- 1 tablespoon olive oil
- 1 1/2 tablespoons cumin
- 1 onion, diced
- 1 teaspoon paprika
- 2 cloves garlic, minced
- 1 teaspoon cayenne pepper
- 1 bell pepper, chopped
- 1 teaspoon chili powder
- 2 (14.5 ounce) cans black beans, rinsed, drained, and mashed
- 1 cup salsa

2 tablespoons yellow cornmeal

DIRECTIONS

1. Heat olive oil in a medium skillet over medium heat. Stir in onion, garlic, and bell pepper; cook until tender. Stir in mashed beans. Add the cornmeal. Mix in cumin, paprika, cayenne, chili powder, and salsa. Cover, and cook 5 minutes.

BROCCOLI SOUP

Servings: 8 | Prep: 15m | Cooks: 25m | Total: 40m

NUTRITION FACTS

Calories: 64 | Carbohydrates: 10.2g | Fat: 2g | Protein: 2.8g | Cholesterol: 0mg

INGREDIENTS

- 1 tablespoon olive oil
- 1 potato, peeled and chopped
- 1 large onion, chopped
- 4 cups chicken broth
- 3 cloves garlic, peeled and chopped
- 1/4 teaspoon ground nutmeg
- 2 (10 ounce) packages chopped frozen broccoli, thawed

salt and pepper to taste**DIRECTIONS**

1. Heat olive oil in a large saucepan, and saute onion and garlic until tender. Mix in broccoli, potato, and chicken broth. Bring to a boil, reduce heat, and simmer 15 minutes, until vegetables are tender.
2. With a hand mixer or in a blender, puree the mixture until smooth. Return to the saucepan, and reheat. Season with nutmeg, salt, and pepper.

CHINESE CHICKEN SALAD

Servings: 4 | Prep: 30m | Cooks: 30m | Total: 1h

NUTRITION FACTS

Calories: 393 | Carbohydrates: 41.9g | Fat: 10.3g | Protein: 34.1g | Cholesterol: 69mg

INGREDIENTS

- 3 tablespoons hoisin sauce
- 1 pound skinless, boneless chicken breast halves
- 2 tablespoons peanut butter
- 16 (3.5 inch square) wonton wrappers, shredded
- 2 teaspoons brown sugar
- 4 cups romaine lettuce - torn, washed and dried
- 3/4 teaspoon hot chile paste
- 2 cups shredded carrots
- 1 teaspoon grated fresh ginger
- 1 bunch green onions, chopped
- 3 tablespoons rice wine vinegar
- 1/4 cup chopped fresh cilantro

1 tablespoon sesame oil

DIRECTIONS

1. To prepare the dressing, whisk together the hoisin sauce, peanut butter, brown sugar, chili paste, ginger, vinegar, and sesame oil.
2. Grill or broil the chicken breasts until cooked, about 10 minutes. An instant-read thermometer inserted into the center should read 165 degrees F (74 degrees C). Cool and slice.
3. Preheat oven to 350 degrees F (175 C). Spray a large shallow pan with nonstick vegetable spray; arrange shredded wontons in a single layer and bake until golden brown, about 20 minutes. Cool.
4. In a large bowl, combine the chicken, wontons, lettuce, carrots, green onions and cilantro. Toss with dressing and serve.

SPICED SLOW COOKER APPLESAUCE

Servings: 8 | Prep: 10m | Cooks: 6h30m | Total: 6h40m

NUTRITION FACTS

Calories: 150 | Carbohydrates: 39.4g | Fat: 0.2g | Protein: 0.4g | Cholesterol: 0mg

INGREDIENTS

- 8 apples - peeled, cored, and thinly sliced
- 3/4 cup packed brown sugar
- 1/2 cup water

1/2 teaspoon pumpkin pie spice**DIRECTIONS**

1. Combine the apples and water in a slow cooker; cook on Low for 6 to 8 hours. Stir in the brown sugar and pumpkin pie spice; continue cooking another 30 minutes.

MEDITERRANEAN KALE
Serving 6 | Prep: 15m | Cooks: 10m | Total: 25m

NUTRITION FACTS

Calories: 91 | Carbohydrates: 14.5g | Fat: 3.2g | Protein: 4.6g | Cholesterol: 0mg

INGREDIENTS

- 12 cups chopped kale
- 1 teaspoon soy sauce
- 2 tablespoons lemon juice
- salt to taste
- 1 tablespoon olive oil, or as needed
- ground black pepper to taste

1 tablespoon minced garlic

DIRECTIONS

1. Place a steamer insert into a saucepan, and fill with water to just below the bottom of the steamer. Cover, and bring the water to a boil over high heat. Add the kale, recover, and steam until just tender, 7 to 10 minutes depending on thickness.
2. Whisk together the lemon juice, olive oil, garlic, soy sauce, salt, and black pepper in a large bowl. Toss steamed kale into dressing until well coated.

CAJUN STYLE BAKED SWEET POTATO
Servings: 4 | Prep: 10m | Cooks: 1h | Total: 1h10m

NUTRITION FACTS

Calories: 229 | Carbohydrates: 49.1g | Fat: 2.3g | Protein: 4.8g | Cholesterol: 0mg

INGREDIENTS

- 1 1/2 teaspoons paprika

- 1/4 teaspoon dried rosemary
- 1 teaspoon brown sugar
- 1/4 teaspoon garlic powder
- 1/4 teaspoon black pepper
- 1/8 teaspoon cayenne pepper
- 1/4 teaspoon onion powder
- 2 large sweet potatoes
- 1/4 teaspoon dried thyme

1 1/2 teaspoons olive oil**DIRECTIONS**

1. Preheat oven to 375 degrees F (190 degrees C).
2. In a small bowl, stir together paprika, brown sugar, black pepper, onion powder, thyme, rosemary, garlic powder, and cayenne pepper.
3. Slice the sweet potatoes in half lengthwise. Brush each half with olive oil. Rub the seasoning mix over the cut surface of each half. Place sweet potatoes on a baking sheet, or in a shallow pan.
4. Bake in preheated oven until tender, or about 1 hour.

ONE SKILLET MEXICAN QUINOA
Servings: 4 | Prep: 15m | Cooks: 25m | Total: 40m

NUTRITION FACTS

Calories: 405 | Carbohydrates: 47.1g | Fat: 14.9g | Protein: 16.5g | Cholesterol: 2mg

INGREDIENTS

- 1 tablespoon olive oil
- 1 tablespoon red pepper flakes, or to taste
- 1 jalapeno pepper, chopped
- 1 1/2 teaspoons chili powder
- 2 cloves garlic, chopped
- 1/2 teaspoon cumin
- 1 (15 ounce) can black beans, rinsed and drained
- 1 pinch kosher salt and ground black pepper to taste
- 1 (14.5 ounce) can fire-roasted diced tomatoes
- 1 avocado - peeled, pitted, and diced
- 1 cup yellow corn
- 1 lime, juiced
- 1 cup quinoa
- 2 tablespoons chopped fresh cilantro

1 cup chicken broth

DIRECTIONS

1. Heat oil in a large skillet over medium-high heat. Saute jalapeno pepper and garlic in hot oil until fragrant, about 1 minute.
2. Stir black beans, tomatoes, yellow corn, quinoa, and chicken broth into skillet; season with red pepper flakes, chili powder, cumin, salt, and black pepper. Bring to a boil, cover the skillet with a lid, reduce heat to low, and simmer until quinoa is tender and liquid is mostly absorbed, about 20 minutes. Stir avocado, lime juice, and cilantro into quinoa until combined.

CREAMY ITALIAN WHITE BEAN SOUP
Servings: 4 | Prep: 20m | Cooks: 30m | Total: 50m

NUTRITION FACTS

Calories: 245 | Carbohydrates: 38.1g | Fat: 4.9g | Protein: 12g | Cholesterol: 2mg

INGREDIENTS

- 1 tablespoon vegetable oil
- 1/4 teaspoon ground black pepper
- 1 onion, chopped
- 1/8 teaspoon dried thyme
- 1 stalk celery, chopped
- 2 cups water
- 1 clove garlic, minced
- 1 bunch fresh spinach, rinsed and thinly sliced
- 2 (16 ounce) cans white kidney beans, rinsed and drained
- 1 tablespoon lemon juice

1 (14 ounce) can chicken broth**DIRECTIONS**

1. In a large saucepan, heat oil. Cook onion and celery in oil for 5 to 8 minutes, or until tender. Add garlic, and cook for 30 seconds, continually stirring. Stir in beans, chicken broth, pepper, thyme and 2 cups water. Bring to a boil, reduce heat, and then simmer for 15 minutes.
2. With slotted spoon, remove 2 cups of the bean and vegetable mixture from soup and set aside.
3. In blender at low speed, blend remaining soup in small batches until smooth, (it helps to remove the center piece of the blender lid to allow steam to escape.) Once blended pour soup back into stock pot and stir in reserved beans.
4. Bring to a boil, occasionally stirring. Stir in spinach and cook 1 minute or until spinach is wilted. Stir in lemon juice and remove from heat and serve with fresh grated Parmesan cheese on top.

TURKEY CARCASS SOUP
Servings: 12 | Prep: 45m | Cooks: 2h | Total: 2h45m

NUTRITION FACTS

Calories: 133 | Carbohydrates: 27.7g | Fat: 1.3g | Protein: 4.2g | Cholesterol: 2mg

INGREDIENTS

- 1 turkey carcass
- 1 tablespoon Worcestershire sauce
- 4 quarts water
- 1 1/2 teaspoons salt
- 6 small potatoes, diced
- 1 teaspoon dried parsley
- 4 large carrots, diced
- 1 teaspoon dried basil
- 2 stalks celery, diced
- 1 bay leaf
- 1 large onion, diced
- 1/4 teaspoon freshly cracked black pepper
- 1 1/2 cups shredded cabbage
- 1/4 teaspoon paprika
- 1 (28 ounce) can whole peeled tomatoes, chopped
- 1/4 teaspoon poultry seasoning
- 1/2 cup uncooked barley

1 pinch dried thyme**DIRECTIONS**

1. Place the turkey carcass into a large soup pot or stock pot and pour in the water; bring to a boil, reduce heat to a simmer, and cook the turkey frame until the remaining meat falls off the bones, about 1 hour. Remove the turkey carcass and remove and chop any remaining turkey meat. Chop the meat.

2. Strain the broth through a fine mesh strainer into a clean soup pot. Add the chopped turkey to the strained broth; bring the to a boil, reduce heat, and stir in the potatoes, carrots, celery, onion, cabbage, tomatoes, barley, Worcestershire sauce, salt, parsley, basil, bay leaf, black pepper, paprika, poultry seasoning, and thyme. Simmer until the vegetables are tender, about 1 more hour. Remove bay leaf before serving.

SUNDAY BEST FRUIT SALAD
Servings: 8 | Prep: 20m | Cooks: 25m | Total: 45m

NUTRITION FACTS

Calories: 183 | Carbohydrates: 45.6g | Fat: 0.5g | Protein: 2.1g | Cholesterol: 0mg

INGREDIENTS

- 1 (20 ounce) can pineapple chunks, juice reserved

- 2 bananas, peeled and diced
- 2 apples, peeled and cored
- 3 kiwis
- 1 (21 ounce) can peach pie filling

1 pint strawberries**DIRECTIONS**

1. In a small bowl, toss the chopped apples in reserved pineapple juice. Allow to sit for 5 to 10 minutes.
2. In a large salad bowl, combine the peach pie filling and pineapple chunks.
3. Remove apples from pineapple juice and add to pie filling and pineapple mixture. Add chopped bananas to reserved pineapple juice and let sit for 5 to 10 minutes.
4. Peel and slice kiwi and 1/2 of strawberries. Chop the other 1/2 of strawberries and set aside.
5. Remove bananas from pineapple juice and add to pie filling mixture. Add chopped strawberries; toss together.
6. Arrange kiwi slices around the edge of the serving bowl and alternate with strawberry slices. Chill and serve.

HONEY ORANGE GREEN BEANS
Servings: 4 | Prep: 20m | Cooks: 25m | Total: 45m

NUTRITION FACTS

Calories: 145 | Carbohydrates: 28.2g | Fat: 1.6g | Protein: 5.2g | Cholesterol: 4mg**INGREDIENTS**

- 3 russet potatoes, sliced into 1/4 inch strips
- 1/4 cup grated Parmesan cheese
- cooking spray
- salt and pepper to taste

1 teaspoon dried basil

DIRECTIONS

1. Preheat oven to 400 degrees F (200 degrees C). Lightly grease a medium baking sheet.
2. Arrange potato strips in a single layer on the prepared baking sheet, skin sides down. Spray lightly with cooking spray, and sprinkle with basil, Parmesan cheese, salt and pepper.
3. Bake 25 minutes in the preheated oven, or until golden brown.

SUPERFAST ASPARAGUS
Servings: 3 | Prep: 5m | Cooks: 10m | Total: 15m

NUTRITION FACTS

Calories: 32 | Carbohydrates: 6.3g | Fat: 0.2g | Protein: 3.4g | Cholesterol: 0mg

INGREDIENTS

- 1 pound asparagus

1 teaspoon Cajun seasoning**DIRECTIONS**

1. Preheat oven to 425 degrees F (220 degrees C).
2. Snap the asparagus at the tender part of the stalk. Arrange spears in one layer on a baking sheet. Spray lightly with nonstick spray; sprinkle with the Cajun seasoning.
3. Bake in the preheated oven until tender, about 10 minutes.

OVEN ROASTED RED POTATOES AND ASPARAGUS
Servings: 6 | Prep: 15m | Cooks: 45m | Total: 1h

NUTRITION FACTS

Calories: 149 | Carbohydrates: 23.5g | Fat: 4.9g | Protein: 4.2g | Cholesterol: 0mg

INGREDIENTS

- 1 1/2 pounds red potatoes, cut into chunks
- 4 teaspoons dried thyme
- 2 tablespoons extra virgin olive oil
- 2 teaspoons kosher salt
- 8 cloves garlic, thinly sliced
- 1 bunch fresh asparagus, trimmed and cut into 1 inch pieces
- 4 teaspoons dried rosemary

ground black pepper to taste**DIRECTIONS**

1. Preheat oven to 425 degrees F (220 degrees C).
2. In a large baking dish, toss the red potatoes with 1/2 the olive oil, garlic, rosemary, thyme, and 1/2 the kosher salt. Cover with aluminum foil.
3. Bake 20 minutes in the preheated oven. Mix in the asparagus, remaining olive oil, and remaining salt. Cover, and continue cooking 15 minutes, or until the potatoes are tender. Increase oven temperature to 450 degrees F (230 degrees C). Remove foil, and continue cooking 5 to 10 minutes, until potatoes are lightly browned. Season with pepper to serve.

CHICKEN ENCHILADA SLOW COOKER SOUP
Servings: 6 | Prep: 15m | Cooks: 6h30m | Total: 6h45m

NUTRITION FACTS

Calories: 186 | Carbohydrates: 22.9g | Fat: 3.4g | Protein: 18.4`g | Cholesterol: 39mg

INGREDIENTS

- 1 pound skinless, boneless chicken breast halves
- 1/4 cup chopped fresh cilantro
- 1 (15.25 ounce) can whole kernel corn, drained
- 2 bay leaves
- 1 (14.5 ounce) can diced tomatoes including juice
- 3 cloves garlic, minced
- 1 (14.5 ounce) can chicken broth
- 1 teaspoon ground cumin
- 1 (10 ounce) can enchilada sauce
- 1 teaspoon chili powder
- 1 (4 ounce) can diced green chiles
- 1 teaspoon salt
- 1 white onion, chopped
- 1/4 teaspoon ground black pepper, or to taste

DIRECTIONS

1. Rinse and pat dry the chicken breasts, then place into the bottom of a slow cooker. Add the corn, tomatoes, chicken broth, enchilada sauce, green chiles, onion, cilantro, bay leaves, garlic, cumin, chili powder, salt, and black pepper.
2. Cook on Low for 6 hours. Transfer the chicken to a large plate, then shred the meat with two forks. Return the chicken to the slow cooker and continue cooking for 30 minutes to 1 hour.

QUINOA WITH CHICKPEAS AND TOMATOES
Servings: 6 | Prep: 20m | Cooks: 20m | Total: 40m

NUTRITION FACTS

Calories: 185 | Carbohydrates: 28.8g | Fat: 5.4g | Protein: 6g | Cholesterol: 0mg

INGREDIENTS

- 1 cup quinoa
- 3 tablespoons lime juice
- 1/8 teaspoon salt
- 4 teaspoons olive oil
- 1 3/4 cups water
- 1/2 teaspoon ground cumin
- 1 cup canned garbanzo beans (chickpeas), drained
- 1 pinch salt and pepper to taste

- 1 tomato, chopped
- 1/2 teaspoon chopped fresh parsley

1 clove garlic, minced

DIRECTIONS

1. Place the quinoa in a fine mesh strainer, and rinse under cold, running water until the water no longer foams. Bring the quinoa, salt, and water to a boil in a saucepan. Reduce heat to medium-low, cover, and simmer until the quinoa is tender, 20 to 25 minutes.
2. Once done, stir in the garbanzo beans, tomatoes, garlic, lime juice, and olive oil. Season with cumin, salt, and pepper. Sprinkle with chopped fresh parsley to serve.

JAMIE'S SWEET AND EASY CORN ON THE COB
Servings: 6 | Prep: 5m | Cooks: 10m | Total: 15m

NUTRITION FACTS

Calories: 94 | Carbohydrates: 21.5g | Fat: 1.1g | Protein: 2.9g | Cholesterol: 0mg

INGREDIENTS

- 2 tablespoons white sugar
- 6 ears corn on the cob, husks and silk removed

1 tablespoon lemon juice

DIRECTIONS

1. Fill a large pot about 3/4 full of water and bring to a boil. Stir in sugar and lemon juice, dissolving the sugar. Gently place ears of corn into boiling water, cover the pot, turn off the heat, and let the corn cook in the hot water until tender, about 10 minutes.

CREAMY ITALIAN WHITE BEAN SOUP
Servings: 4 | Prep: 20m | Cooks: 30m | Total: 50m

NUTRITION FACTS

Calories: 245 | Carbohydrates: 38.1g | Fat: 4.9g | Protein: 12g | Cholesterol: 2mg

INGREDIENTS

- 1 tablespoon vegetable oil
- 1/4 teaspoon ground black pepper

- 1 onion, chopped
- 1/8 teaspoon dried thyme
- 1 stalk celery, chopped
- 2 cups water
- 1 clove garlic, minced
- 1 bunch fresh spinach, rinsed and thinly sliced
- 2 (16 ounce) cans white kidney beans, rinsed and drained
- 1 tablespoon lemon juice

1 (14 ounce) can chicken broth

DIRECTIONS

1. In a large saucepan, heat oil. Cook onion and celery in oil for 5 to 8 minutes, or until tender. Add garlic, and cook for 30 seconds, continually stirring. Stir in beans, chicken broth, pepper, thyme and 2 cups water. Bring to a boil, reduce heat, and then simmer for 15 minutes.
2. With slotted spoon, remove 2 cups of the bean and vegetable mixture from soup and set aside.
3. In blender at low speed, blend remaining soup in small batches until smooth, (it helps to remove the center piece of the blender lid to allow steam to escape.) Once blended pour soup back into stock pot and stir in reserved beans.
4. Bring to a boil, occasionally stirring. Stir in spinach and cook 1 minute or until spinach is wilted. Stir in lemon juice and remove from heat and serve with fresh grated Parmesan cheese on top.

TURKEY CARCASS SOUP
Servings: 12 | Prep: 45m | Cooks: 2h | Total: 2h45m

NUTRITION FACTS

Calories: 133 | Carbohydrates: 27.7g | Fat: 1.3g | Protein: 4.2g | Cholesterol: 2mg

INGREDIENTS

- 1 turkey carcass
- 1 tablespoon Worcestershire sauce
- 4 quarts water
- 1 1/2 teaspoons salt
- 6 small potatoes, diced
- 1 teaspoon dried parsley
- 4 large carrots, diced
- 1 teaspoon dried basil
- 2 stalks celery, diced
- 1 bay leaf
- 1 large onion, diced
- 1/4 teaspoon freshly cracked black pepper
- 1 1/2 cups shredded cabbage

- 1/4 teaspoon paprika
- 1 (28 ounce) can whole peeled tomatoes, chopped
- 1/4 teaspoon poultry seasoning
- 1/2 cup uncooked barley
- 1 pinch dried thyme
- 1 turkey carcass

1 tablespoon Worcestershire sauce**DIRECTIONS**

1. Place the turkey carcass into a large soup pot or stock pot and pour in the water; bring to a boil, reduce heat to a simmer, and cook the turkey frame until the remaining meat falls off the bones, about 1 hour. Remove the turkey carcass and remove and chop any remaining turkey meat. Chop the meat.

2. Strain the broth through a fine mesh strainer into a clean soup pot. Add the chopped turkey to the strained broth; bring the to a boil, reduce heat, and stir in the potatoes, carrots, celery, onion, cabbage, tomatoes, barley, Worcestershire sauce, salt, parsley, basil, bay leaf, black pepper, paprika, poultry seasoning, and thyme. Simmer until the vegetables are tender, about 1 more hour. Remove bay leaf before serving.

MOROCCAN CHICKEN
Servings: 4 | Prep: 10m | Cooks: 30m | Total: 45m | Additional: 5m

NUTRITION FACTS

Calories: 286 | Carbohydrates: 27.9g | Fat: 3.7g | Protein: 36g | Cholesterol: 67mg

INGREDIENTS

- 1 pound skinless, boneless chicken breast meat - cubed
- 3/4 teaspoon ground cumin
- 2 teaspoons salt
- 1/2 teaspoon dried oregano
- 1 onion, chopped
- 1/4 teaspoon ground cayenne pepper
- 2 cloves garlic, chopped
- 1/4 teaspoon ground turmeric
- 2 carrots, sliced
- 1 1/2 cups chicken broth
- 2 stalks celery, sliced
- 1 cup crushed tomatoes
- 1 tablespoon minced fresh ginger root
- 1 cup canned chickpeas, drained

½ teaspoon paprika

DIRECTIONS

1. Season chicken with salt and brown in a large saucepan over medium heat until almost cooked through. Remove chicken from pan and set aside.
2. Saute onion, garlic, carrots and celery in same pan. When tender, stir in ginger, paprika, cumin, oregano, cayenne pepper and turmeric; stir fry for about 1 minute, then mix in broth and tomatoes. Return chicken to pan, reduce heat to low and simmer for about 10 minutes.
3. Add chickpeas and zucchini to pan and bring to simmering once again; cover pan and cook for about 15 minutes, or until zucchini is cooked through and tender. Stir in lemon juice and serve.

CROCK-POT CHICKEN CHILI
Servings: 5 | Prep: 10m | Cooks: 6h | Total: 6h10m

NUTRITION FACTS

Calories: 386 | Carbohydrates: 62.9g | Fat: 2.9g | Protein: 28.8g | Cholesterol: 37mg

INGREDIENTS

- 1 (16 ounce) jar green salsa (salsa verde)
- 1 onion, chopped
- 1 (16 ounce) can diced tomatoes with green chile peppers
- 1/2 teaspoon dried oregano
- 2 (15 ounce) cans white beans, drained
- 1/4 teaspoon ground cumin
- 1 (14.5 ounce) can chicken broth
- salt and ground black pepper to taste
- 1 (14 ounce) can corn, drained

3 skinless, boneless chicken breasts**DIRECTIONS**

1. Mix green salsa, diced tomatoes with green chile peppers, white beans, chicken broth, corn, onion, oregano, cumin, salt, and black pepper together in a slow cooker. Lay chicken breasts atop the mixture.
2. Cook on Low until the chicken shreds easily with 2 forks, 6 to 8 hours.
3. Remove chicken to a cutting board and shred completely; return to chili in slow cooker and stir.

SPINACH LENTIL SOUP
Servings: 8 | Prep: 15m | Cooks: 35m | Total: 50m

NUTRITION FACTS

Calories: 150 | Carbohydrates: 22.7g | Fat: 2.4g | Protein: 10.1g | Cholesterol: 10mg

INGREDIENTS

- 1/3 cup uncooked white rice
- 1/2 teaspoon crushed red pepper flakes
- 2/3 cup water
- 6 cups water
- 1 teaspoon vegetable oil
- 2 cups reduced sodium chicken broth
- 4 ounces turkey kielbasa, chopped
- 1 cup dry lentils
- 1 onion, minced
- 1 (10 ounce) bag fresh spinach, torn

1 carrot, chopped**DIRECTIONS**

1. In a pot, bring the rice and water to a boil. Reduce heat to low, cover, and simmer 20 minutes.
2. Heat the oil in a large pot over medium heat, and cook the turkey kielbasa until lightly browned. Mix in onion and carrot, and season with red pepper. Cook and stir until tender. Pour in the water and broth, and mix in lentils. Bring to a boil, reduce heat to low, and simmer 25 minutes.
3. Stir the cooked rice and spinach into the soup, and continue cooking 5 minutes before serving.

CARROT, POTATO, AND CABBAGE SOUP
Servings: 6 | Prep: 30m | Cooks: 20m | Total: 50m

NUTRITION FACTS

Calories: 161 | Carbohydrates: 31.3g | Fat: 3.1g | Protein: 3.8g | Cholesterol: < 1mg

INGREDIENTS

- 4 large carrots, thinly sliced
- 1 tablespoon olive oil
- 2 large potatoes, thinly sliced
- 1/4 teaspoon dried thyme
- 1 large onion, thinly sliced
- 1/4 teaspoon dried basil
- 1/4 medium head green cabbage, thinly sliced
- 1 teaspoon dried parsley
- 2 cloves garlic, smashed
- 1 teaspoon salt
- 6 cups chicken stock

ground black pepper to taste**DIRECTIONS**

1. Combine the carrots, potatoes, onion, cabbage, garlic, chicken stock, olive oil, thyme, basil, parsley, salt, and pepper in a stock pot over medium-high heat; bring to a simmer and cook until the carrots are tender, about 20 minutes. Transfer to a blender in small batches and blend until smooth.

MAKE-AHEAD VEGETARIAN MOROCCAN STEW
Servings: 6 | Prep: 30m | Cooks: 40m | Total: 1h10m

NUTRITION FACTS

Calories: 543 | Carbohydrates: 110.6g | Fat: 4.2g | Protein: 19.5g | Cholesterol: 5mg**INGREDIENTS**

- 1 teaspoon ground cinnamon
- 1 (15 ounce) can garbanzo beans, drained
- 1 teaspoon ground cumin
- 1 (14.5 ounce) can diced tomatoes, undrained
- 1 teaspoon kosher salt
- 3 large potatoes, peeled and diced
- 1/2 teaspoon ground ginger
- 2 sweet potatoes, peeled and diced
- 1/4 teaspoon ground cloves
- 4 large carrots, chopped
- 1/4 teaspoon ground nutmeg
- 1 cup dried lentils, rinsed
- 1/4 teaspoon ground turmeric
- 1/2 cup chopped dried apricots
- 1/8 teaspoon curry powder
- 1 tablespoon honey
- 1 tablespoon butter
- 1 teaspoon ground black pepper, to taste
- 1 sweet onion, chopped
- 1 tablespoon cornstarch (optional)
- 2 cups finely shredded kale
- 1 tablespoon water (optional)

4 (14 ounce) cans organic vegetable broth

DIRECTIONS

1. Combine cinnamon, cumin, salt, ginger, cloves, nutmeg, turmeric, and curry powder in a large bowl.
2. Melt butter in a large pot over medium heat. Cook the onion in the butter until soft and just beginning to brown, 5 to 10 minutes. Stir in kale and spice mixture; cook until kale begins to wilt and spices are fragrant, about 2 minutes.

3. Pour the vegetable broth into the pot. Stir garbanzo beans, tomatoes, potatoes, sweet potatoes, carrots, lentils, apricots, and honey, into the broth; bring to boil, reduce heat to low, and simmer until vegetables and lentils are cooked and tender, about 30 minutes. Season stew with black pepper.

4. Dissolve cornstarch in water; stir into stew and simmer thickened, about 5 minutes.

BLACK BEAN CHILI
Servings: 8 | Prep: 20m | Cooks: 20m | Total: 40m

NUTRITION FACTS

Calories: 164 | Carbohydrates: 28g | Fat: 2.8g | Protein: 9g | Cholesterol: < 1mg**INGREDIENTS**

- 1 tablespoon olive oil
- 1 teaspoon ground black pepper
- 1 onion, chopped
- 1 teaspoon ground cumin
- 2 red bell pepper, seeded and chopped
- 1 tablespoon chili powder
- 1 jalapeno pepper, seeded and minced
- 2 (15 ounce) cans black beans, drained and rinsed
- 10 fresh mushrooms, quartered
- 1 1/2 cups chicken broth or vegetable broth
- 6 roma (plum) tomatoes, diced
- 1 teaspoon salt

1 cup fresh corn kernels

DIRECTIONS

1. Heat oil in a large saucepan over medium-high heat. Saute the onion, red bell peppers, jalapeno, mushrooms, tomatoes and corn for 10 minutes or until the onions are translucent. Season with black pepper, cumin, and chili powder. Stir in the black beans, chicken or vegetable broth, and salt. Bring to a boil.

2. Reduce heat to medium low. Remove 1 1/2 cups of the soup to food processor or blender; puree and stir the bean mixture back into the soup. Serve hot by itself or over rice.

SPLIT PEA SOUP WITH ROSEMARY
Servings: 6 | Prep: 20m | Cooks: 1h15m | Total: 1h35m

NUTRITION FACTS

Calories: 253 | Carbohydrates: 35.5g | Fat: 5g | Protein: 17g | Cholesterol: 15mg

INGREDIENTS

- 6 slices bacon, cut into 1 inch pieces
- 4 (10.5 ounce) cans chicken broth
- 1 small onion, chopped
- 1 1/2 cups green split peas
- 1 leek, thinly sliced
- 2 bay leaves
- 1 large carrot, chopped
- 1 teaspoon chopped fresh rosemary

2 cloves garlic, minced

DIRECTIONS

1. Place bacon in a large pot, and cook over medium heat until crisp. Stir in onion, leek, carrot, and garlic; cook until the vegetables are soft, about 8 minutes. Pour in chicken broth. Stir in split peas, bay leaves, and rosemary. Bring to a boil. Reduce heat to low; cover, and simmer until peas are cooked, about 1 hour, stirring occasionally.

OVEN FRIES
Servings: 6 | Prep: 15m | Cooks: 30m | Total: 45m

NUTRITION FACTS

Calories: 156 | Carbohydrates: 34.1g | Fat: 1g | Protein: 3.8g | Cholesterol: 0mg

INGREDIENTS

- 2 1/2 pounds baking potatoes
- 1 teaspoon salt
- 1 teaspoon vegetable oil
- 1 pinch ground cayenne pepper

1 tablespoon white sugar

DIRECTIONS

1. Preheat oven to 450 degrees F (230 degrees C). Line a baking sheet with foil, and coat well with vegetable cooking spray. Scrub potatoes well and cut into 1/2 inch thick fries.
2. In a large mixing bowl, toss potatoes with oil, sugar, salt and red pepper. Spread on baking sheet in one layer.
3. Bake for 30 minutes in the preheated oven, until potatoes are tender and browned. Serve immediately.

BAKED BEANS, TEXAS RANGER

Servings: 6 | Prep: 15m | Cooks: 1h | Total: 1h15m

NUTRITION FACTS

Calories: 301 | Carbohydrates: 55.7g | Fat: 6.1g | Protein: 10.8g | Cholesterol: 23mg**INGREDIENTS**

- 1 (28 ounce) can baked beans with pork
- 4 tablespoons vinegar
- 1 medium onion, diced
- 1/2 cup packed brown sugar
- 1 medium bell pepper, diced
- 1/2 cup ketchup
- 4 links spicy pork sausage, cut into chunks
- 1 teaspoon garlic powder
- 2 tablespoons chili powder
- salt to taste
- 3 tablespoons Worcestershire sauce

1 dash cayenne pepper (optional)**DIRECTIONS**

1. Preheat the oven to 350 degrees F (175 degrees C).
2. In a Dutch oven, combine the baked beans, onion, bell pepper, and sausage. Season with chili powder, Worcestershire sauce, vinegar, brown sugar, ketchup, garlic powder and salt. Add a dash of cayenne if desired.
3. Cover and bake for one hour in the preheated oven.

ROASTED YAM AND KALE SALAD

Servings: 6 | Prep: 20m | Cooks: 20m | Total: 1h15m

NUTRITION FACTS

Calories: 274 | Carbohydrates: 49.2g | Fat: 7.5g | Protein: 5g | Cholesterol: 0mg

INGREDIENTS

- 2 jewel yams, cut into 1-inch cubes
- 3 cloves garlic, minced
- 2 tablespoons olive oil
- 1 bunch kale, torn into bite-sized pieces
- salt and freshly ground black pepper to taste
- 2 tablespoons red wine vinegar
- 1 tablespoon olive oil
- 1 teaspoon chopped fresh thyme

1 onion, sliced**DIRECTIONS**

1. Preheat an oven to 400 degrees F (200 degrees C). Toss the yams with 2 tablespoons of olive oil in a bowl. Season to taste with salt and pepper, and arrange evenly onto a baking sheet.
2. Bake in the preheated oven until the yams are tender, 20 to 25 minutes. Cool to room temperature in the refrigerator.
3. Meanwhile, heat the remaining 1 tablespoon of olive oil in a large skillet over medium heat. Cook and stir the onion and garlic until the onion has caramelized to a golden brown, about 15 minutes. Stir in the kale, cooking until wilted and tender. Transfer the kale mixture to a bowl, and cool to room temperature in the refrigerator.
4. Once all the ingredients have cooled, combine the yams, kale, red wine vinegar, and fresh thyme in a bowl. Season to taste with salt and pepper, and gently stir to combine.

SLOW COOKER VEGETARIAN MINESTRONE

Servings: 8 | Prep: 20m | Cooks: 6h15m | Total: 6h35m

NUTRITION FACTS

Calories: 138 | Carbohydrates: 25.2g | Fat: 1.7g | Protein: 6.9g | Cholesterol: 2mg

INGREDIENTS

- 6 cups vegetable broth
- 1 tablespoon minced fresh parsley
- 1 (28 ounce) can crushed tomatoes
- 1 1/2 teaspoons dried oregano
- 1 (15 ounce) can kidney beans, drained
- 1 teaspoon salt
- 1 large onion, chopped
- 3/4 teaspoon dried thyme
- 2 ribs celery, diced
- 1/4 teaspoon freshly ground black pepper
- 2 large carrots, diced
- 1/2 cup elbow macaroni
- 1 cup green beans
- 4 cups chopped fresh spinach
- 1 small zucchini
- 1/4 cup finely grated Parmesan cheese, or more to taste

3 cloves garlic, minced

DIRECTIONS

1. Combine vegetable broth, tomatoes, kidney beans, onion, celery, carrots, green beans, zucchini, garlic, parsley, oregano, salt, thyme, and black pepper in a 6-quart slow cooker.
2. Cook on Low for 6 to 8 hours.

3. Bring a large pot of lightly salted water to a boil. Cook elbow macaroni in the boiling water, stirring occasionally until cooked through but firm to the bite, 8 minutes; drain.

4. Stir spinach and macaroni into minestrone; cook another 15 minutes. Top with Parmesan cheese.

CALDO DE RES (MEXICAN BEEF SOUP)

Servings: 8 | Prep: 30m | Cooks: 2h | Total: 2h30m

NUTRITION FACTS

Calories: 234 | Carbohydrates: 25.9g | Fat: 5.7g | Protein: 22g | Cholesterol: 39mg

INGREDIENTS

- 2 pounds beef shank, with bone
- 1 potato, quartered (optional)
- 1 tablespoon vegetable oil
- 2 ears corn, husked and cut into thirds
- 2 teaspoons salt
- 2 chayotes, quartered (optional)
- 2 teaspoons ground black pepper
- 1 medium head cabbage, cored and cut into wedges
- 1 onion, chopped
- 1/4 cup sliced pickled jalapenos
- 1 (14.5 ounce) can diced tomatoes
- ¼ cup finely chopped onion
- 3 cups beef broth
- 1 cup chopped fresh cilantro
- 4 cups water
- 2 limes, cut into wedges
- 2 medium carrot, coarsely chopped
- 4 radishes, quartered

1/4 cup chopped fresh cilantro

DIRECTIONS

1. Cut the meat from the beef bones into about 1/2 inch pieces, leaving some on the bones.
2. Heat a heavy soup pot over medium-high heat until very hot. Add the oil, tilting the pan to coat the bottom. Add the meat and bones, and season with salt and pepper. Cook and stir until thoroughly browned.
3. Add 1 onion, and cook until onion is also lightly browned. Stir in the tomatoes and broth. The liquid should cover the bones by 1/2 inch. If not, add enough water to compensate. Reduce heat to low, and

simmer for 1 hour with the lid on loosely. If meat is not tender, continue cooking for another 10 minutes or so.

4. Pour in the water, and return to a simmer. Add the carrot and 1/4 cup cilantro, and cook for 10 minutes, then stir in the potato, corn and chayote. Simmer until vegetables are tender. Push the cabbage wedges into the soup, and cook for about 10 more minutes.
5. Ladle soup into large bowls, including meat vegetables and bones. Garnish with jalapenos, minced onion, and additional cilantro. Squeeze lime juice over all, and serve with radishes.

VINTAGE LEMONADE
Servings: 4 | Prep: 45m | Cooks: 20m | Total: 1h5m

NUTRITION FACTS

Calories: 269 | Carbohydrates: 76.9g | Fat: 0.4g | Protein: 1.6g | Cholesterol: 0mg

INGREDIENTS

- 5 lemons
- 1 1/4 quarts water

1 1/4 cups white sugar

DIRECTIONS

1. Peel the rinds from the 5 lemons and cut them into 1/2 inch slices. Set the lemons aside.
2. Place the rinds in a bowl and sprinkle the sugar over them. Let this stand for about one hour, so that the sugar begins to soak up the oils from the lemons.
3. Bring water to a boil in a covered saucepan and then pour the hot water over the sugared lemon rinds. Allow this mixture to cool for 20 minutes and then remove the rinds.
4. Squeeze the lemons into another bowl. Pour the juice through a strainer into the sugar mixture. Stir well, pour into pitcher and pop it in the fridge! Serve with ice cubes.

BUTTERNUT SQUASH FRIES
Servings: 4 | Prep: 15m | Cooks: 20m | Total: 35m

NUTRITION FACTS

Calories: 102 | Carbohydrates: 26.5g | Fat: 0.2g | Protein: 2.3g | Cholesterol: 0mg

INGREDIENTS

- 1 (2 pound) butternut squash, halved and seeded
- salt to taste

DIRECTIONS

1. Preheat the oven to 425 degrees F (220 degrees C).
2. Use a sharp knife to carefully cut away the peel from the squash. Cut the squash into sticks like French fries. Arrange squash pieces on a baking sheet and season with salt.
3. Bake for 20 minutes in the preheated oven, turning the fries over halfway through baking. Fries are done when they are starting to brown on the edges and become crispy.

VEGGIE VEGETARIAN CHILI

Servings: 16 | Prep: 15m | Cooks: 140m | Total: 55m

NUTRITION FACTS

Calories: 98 | Carbohydrates: 18.5g | Fat: 1.8g | Protein: 4.4g | Cholesterol: 0mg

INGREDIENTS

- 1 tablespoon vegetable oil
- 1 (15 ounce) can black beans, undrained
- 3 cloves garlic, minced
- 1 (15 ounce) can kidney beans, undrained
- 1 cup chopped onion
- 1 (15 ounce) can pinto beans, undrained
- 1 cup chopped carrots
- 1 (15 ounce) can whole kernel corn, drained
- 1 cup chopped green bell pepper
- 1 tablespoon cumin
- 1 cup chopped red bell pepper
- 1 1/2 tablespoons dried oregano
- 2 tablespoons chili powder
- 1 1/2 tablespoons dried basil
- 1 1/2 cups chopped fresh mushrooms
- 1/2 tablespoon garlic powder

1 (28 ounce) can whole peeled tomatoes with liquid, chopped

DIRECTIONS

1. Heat the oil in a large pot over medium heat. Cook and stir the garlic, onion, and carrots in the pot until tender. Mix in the green bell pepper and red bell pepper. Season with chili powder. Continue cooking 5 minutes, or until peppers are tender.
2. Mix the mushrooms into the pot. Stir in the tomatoes with liquid, black beans with liquid, kidney beans with liquid, pinto beans with liquid, and corn. Season with cumin, oregano, basil, and garlic powder. Bring to a boil. Reduce heat to medium, cover, and cook 20 minutes, stirring occasionally.

MEXICAN PASTA

Servings: 4 | Prep: 5m | Cooks: 15m | Total: 20m

NUTRITION FACTS

Calories: 358 | Carbohydrates: 59.5g | Fat: 9.4g | Protein: 10.3g | Cholesterol: 0mg

INGREDIENTS

- 1/2 pound seashell pasta
- 1 (14.5 ounce) can peeled and diced tomatoes
- 2 tablespoons olive oil
- 1/4 cup salsa
- 2 onions, chopped
- 1/4 cup sliced black olives
- 1 green bell pepper, chopped
- 1 1/2 tablespoons taco seasoning mix
- 1/2 cup sweet corn kernels
- salt and pepper to taste

1 (15 ounce) can black beans, drained

DIRECTIONS

1. Bring a large pot of lightly salted water to a boil. Add pasta and cook for 8 to 10 minutes or until al dente; drain.
2. While pasta is cooking, heat olive oil over medium heat in a large skillet. Cook onions and pepper in oil until lightly browned, 10 minutes. Stir in corn and heat through. Stir in black beans, tomatoes, salsa, olives, taco seasoning and salt and pepper and cook until thoroughly heated, 5 minutes.
3. Toss sauce with cooked pasta and serve.

LEBANESE-STYLE RED LENTIL SOUP

Servings: 8 | Prep: 20m | Cooks: 30m | Total: 50m

NUTRITION FACTS

Calories: 276 | Carbohydrates: 39.1g | Fat: 7g | Protein: 16.7g | Cholesterol: 1mg**INGREDIENTS**

- 6 cups chicken stock
- 1 tablespoon ground cumin
- 1 pound red lentils
- 1/2 teaspoon cayenne pepper
- 3 tablespoons olive oil
- 1/2 cup chopped cilantro
- 1 tablespoon minced garlic

- 3/4 cup fresh lemon juice

1 large onion, chopped

DIRECTIONS

1. Bring chicken stock and lentils to a boil in a large saucepan over high heat, then reduce heat to medium-low, cover, and simmer for 20 minutes.
2. Meanwhile, heat olive oil in a skillet over medium heat. Stir in garlic and onion, and cook until the onion has softened and turned translucent, about 3 minutes.
3. Stir onions into the lentils and season with cumin and cayenne. Continue simmering until the lentils are tender, about 10 minutes.
4. Carefully puree the soup in a standing blender, or with a stick blender until smooth. Stir in cilantro and lemon juice before serving.

APRICOT LENTIL SOUP
Servings: 6 | Prep: 15m | Cooks: 50m | Total: 1h55m

NUTRITION FACTS

Calories: 263 | Carbohydrates: 37.2g | Fat: 7.4g | Protein: 13.2g | Cholesterol: 0mg

INGREDIENTS

- 3 tablespoons olive oil
- 3 roma (plum) tomatoes - peeled, seeded and chopped
- 1 onion, chopped
- 1/2 teaspoon ground cumin
- 2 cloves garlic, minced
- 1/2 teaspoon dried thyme
- 1/3 cup dried apricots
- salt to taste
- 1 1/2 cups red lentils
- ground black pepper to taste
- 5 cups chicken stock

2 tablespoons fresh lemon juice**DIRECTIONS**

1. Saute onion, garlic, and apricots in olive oil. Add lentils and stock. Bring to a boil, then reduce heat and simmer 30 minutes.
2. Stir in tomatoes, and season with cumin, thyme, and salt and pepper to taste. Simmer for 10 minutes.
3. Stir in lemon juice. Puree 1/2 of the soup in a blender, then return to the pot. Serve.

ROASTED VEGETABLE MEDLEY
Servings: 6 | Prep: 25m | Cooks: 1h | Total: 1h55m | Additional: 30m

NUTRITION FACTS

Calories: 191 | Carbohydrates: 34.6g | Fat: 5g | Protein: 4g | Cholesterol: 0mg

INGREDIENTS

- 2 tablespoons olive oil, divided
- 1/2 cup roasted red peppers, cut into 1-inch pieces
- 1 large yam, peeled and cut into 1 inch pieces
- 2 cloves garlic, minced
- 1 large parsnip, peeled and cut into 1 inch pieces
- 1/4 cup chopped fresh basil
- 1 cup baby carrots
- 1/2 teaspoon kosher salt
- 1 zucchini, cut into 1 inch slices
- 1/2 teaspoon ground black pepper

1 bunch fresh asparagus, trimmed and cut into 1 inch pieces

DIRECTIONS

1. Preheat oven to 425 degrees F (220 degrees C). Grease 2 baking sheets with 1 tablespoon olive oil.
2. Place the yams, parsnips, and carrots onto the baking sheets. Bake in the preheated oven for 30 minutes, then add the zucchini and asparagus, and drizzle with the remaining 1 tablespoon of olive oil. Continue baking until all of the vegetables are tender, about 30 minutes more. Once tender, remove from the oven, and allow to cool for 30 minutes on the baking sheet.
3. Toss the roasted peppers together with the garlic, basil, salt, and pepper in a large bowl until combined. Add the roasted vegetables, and toss to mix. Serve at room temperature or cold.

MUSHROOM LENTIL BARLEY STEW
Servings: 8 | Prep: 15m | Cooks: 12h | Total: 12h15m

NUTRITION FACTS

Calories: 213 | Carbohydrates: 43.9g | Fat: 1.2g | Protein: 8.4g | Cholesterol: 0mg

INGREDIENTS

- 2 quarts vegetable broth
- 2 teaspoons minced garlic
- 2 cups sliced fresh button mushrooms
- 2 teaspoons dried summer savory
- 1 ounce dried shiitake mushrooms, torn into pieces
- 3 bay leaves

- 3/4 cup uncooked pearl barley
- 1 teaspoon dried basil
- 3/4 cup dry lentils
- 2 teaspoons ground black pepper
- 1/4 cup dried onion flakes

salt to taste**DIRECTIONS**

1. In a slow cooker, mix the broth, button mushrooms, shiitake mushrooms, barley, lentils, onion flakes, garlic, savory, bay leaves, basil, pepper, and salt.
2. Cover, and cook 4 to 6 hours on High or 10 to 12 hours on Low. Remove bay leaves before serving.

SWEET POTATO MINESTRONE
Servings: 6 | Prep: 30m | Cooks: 30m | Total: 1h

NUTRITION FACTS

Calories: 201 | Carbohydrates: 39.9g | Fat: 2.7g | Protein: 4.5g | Cholesterol: 0mg

INGREDIENTS

- 1 tablespoon vegetable oil
- 5 cups vegetable broth
- 1 large onion, chopped
- 2 large sweet potatoes, peeled and diced
- 2 large stalks celery, chopped
- 2 large carrots, sliced thin
- 2 1/2 teaspoons Italian seasoning
- 6 ounces green beans, cut into 1 inch pieces
- salt and pepper to taste
- 5 cloves garlic, minced

1 (28 ounce) can Italian-style diced tomatoes

DIRECTIONS

1. Heat oil in a soup pot over medium-high heat. Saute onion, celery, Italian seasoning, salt and pepper until tender, about 5 minutes. Stir in tomatoes, with the juice, broth, sweet potatoes, carrots, green beans and garlic. Bring to a boil; reduce heat to low and simmer, stirring occasionally, until vegetables are tender, about 30 minutes.

MICHELLE'S BLONDE CHICKEN CHILI
Servings: 10 | Prep: 30m | Cooks: 30m | Total: 1h

NUTRITION FACTS

Calories: 412 | Carbohydrates: 46.6g | Fat: 4.1g | Protein: 47.2g | Cholesterol: 79mg

INGREDIENTS

- 1 tablespoon vegetable oil
- 1 tablespoon garlic powder
- 3 pounds skinless, boneless chicken breast meat - cubed
- 1 tablespoon ground cumin
- 1 cup chopped onion
- 1 tablespoon dried oregano
- 2 cups chicken broth
- 2 teaspoons chopped fresh cilantro
- 2 (4 ounce) cans chopped green chile peppers
- 1 teaspoon crushed red pepper

5 (14.5 ounce) cans great Northern beans, undrained

DIRECTIONS

1. In a large skillet over medium-high heat, place the vegetable oil and chicken. Cook the chicken, stirring occasionally, until all pieces are evenly brown. Stir in the onions. Cook until translucent. Drain mixture and set aside.

2. In a large saucepan over medium heat, bring the chicken broth and green chile peppers to a boil. Stir in 3 cans great northern beans, garlic powder, cumin, oregano, cilantro and crushed red pepper. Stir in the chicken and onion mixture, and reduce heat. Simmer 30 minutes or longer, adding additional beans from the remaining cans for a thicker consistency as desired.

SLOW COOKER HOMEMADE BEANS
Servings: 8 | Prep: 20m | Cooks: 10h | Total: 10h20m

NUTRITION FACTS

Calories: 296 | Carbohydrates: 57g | Fat: 3g | Protein: 12.4g | Cholesterol: 5mg

INGREDIENTS

- 3 cups dry navy beans, soaked overnight or boiled for one hour
- 1 tablespoon dry mustard
- 1 1/2 cups ketchup
- 1 tablespoon salt
- 1 1/2 cups water
- 6 slices thick cut bacon, cut into 1 inch pieces

- 1/4 cup molasses
- 1 cup brown sugar

1 large onion, chopped

DIRECTIONS

1. Drain soaking liquid from beans, and place them in a Slow Cooker.
2. Stir ketchup, water, molasses, onion, mustard, salt, bacon, and brown sugar into the beans until well mixed.
3. Cover, and cook on LOW for 8 to 10 hours, stirring occasionally if possible, though not necessary.

QUICK BLACK BEANS AND RICE
Servings: 4 | Prep: 5m | Cooks: 15m | Total: 25m

NUTRITION FACTS

Calories: 271 | Carbohydrates: 47.8g | Fat: 5.3g | Protein: 10g | Cholesterol: 0mg

INGREDIENTS

- 1 tablespoon vegetable oil
- 1 teaspoon dried oregano
- 1 onion, chopped
- 1/2 teaspoon garlic powder
- 1 (15 ounce) can black beans, undrained
- 1 1/2 cups uncooked instant brown rice

1 (14.5 ounce) can stewed tomatoes

DIRECTIONS

1. In large saucepan, heat oil over medium-high. Add onion, cook and stir until tender. Add beans, tomatoes, oregano and garlic powder. Bring to a boil; stir in rice. Cover; reduce heat and simmer 5 minutes. Remove from heat; let stand 5 minutes before serving.

SPINACH CHICKPEA CURRY
Servings: 4 | Prep: 5m | Cooks: 15m | Total: 20m

NUTRITION FACTS

Calories: 346 | Carbohydrates: 44.7g | Fat: 12.3g | Protein: 21.7g | Cholesterol: 0mg

INGREDIENTS

- 1 tablespoon vegetable oil
- 1/2 teaspoon garlic powder, or to taste
- 1 onion, chopped
- 1 (15 ounce) can garbanzo beans (chickpeas), drained and rinsed
- 1 (14.75 ounce) can creamed corn
- 1 (12 ounce) package firm tofu, cubed
- 1 tablespoon curry paste
- 1 bunch fresh spinach, stems removed
- salt to taste
- 1 teaspoon dried basil or to taste
- ground black pepper to taste

DIRECTIONS

1. In a large wok or skillet heat oil over medium heat; saute onions until translucent. Stir in creamed corn and curry paste. Cook, stirring regularly, for 5 minutes. As you stir, add salt, pepper and garlic.
2. Stir in garbanzo beans and gently fold in tofu. Add spinach and cover. When spinach is tender, remove from heat and stir in basil.

VEGETARIAN CHILI

Servings: 6 | Prep: 10m | Cooks: 1h | Total: 1h10m

NUTRITION FACTS

Calories: 582 | Carbohydrates: 74.2g | Fat: 4.9g | Protein: 67.5g | Cholesterol: 0mg

INGREDIENTS

- 1 (12 ounce) package frozen burger-style crumbles
- 5 onions, chopped
- 2 (15 ounce) cans black beans, rinsed and drained
- 3 tablespoons chili powder
- 2 (15 ounce) cans dark red kidney beans
- 1 1/2 tablespoons ground cumin
- 1 (15 ounce) can light red kidney beans
- 1 tablespoon garlic powder
- 1 (29 ounce) can diced tomatoes
- 2 bay leaves
- 1 (12 fluid ounce) can tomato juice
- salt and pepper to taste

DIRECTIONS

1. In a large pot, combine meat substitute, black beans, kidney beans, diced tomatoes, tomato juice, onions, chili powder, cumin, garlic powder, bay leaves, salt and pepper. Bring to a simmer and cover. Let the chili simmer for at least 1 hour before serving.

APPLESAUCE
Servings: 4 | Prep: 20m | Cooks: 15m | Total: 35m

NUTRITION FACTS

Calories: 195 | Carbohydrates: 51g | Fat: 0.3g | Protein: 0.5g | Cholesterol: 0mg

INGREDIENTS

- 6 cups apples - peeled, cored and chopped
- 1/8 teaspoon ground cloves
- 3/4 cup water
- 1/2 cup white sugar
- 1/8 teaspoon ground cinnamon

DIRECTIONS

1. In a 2 quart saucepan over medium heat, combine apples, water, cinnamon, and cloves. Bring to a boil, reduce heat, and simmer 10 minutes. Stir in sugar, and simmer 5 more minutes.

LENTIL SOUP
Servings: 8 | Prep: 5m | Cooks: 30m | Total: 35m

NUTRITION FACTS

Calories: 156 | Carbohydrates: 27.7g | Fat: 0.7g | Protein: 11.5g | Cholesterol: 0mg

INGREDIENTS

- 2 cups dry lentils
- 1/4 cup tomato paste
- 2 quarts chicken broth
- 2 cloves garlic, minced
- 1 onion, diced
- 1 tablespoon ground cumin

DIRECTIONS

1. In a large saucepan combine lentils, broth, onion, tomato paste, garlic and cumin. Bring to a boil, then reduce heat, cover and simmer until lentils are soft, 30 to 45 minutes. Serve with a squeeze of lemon.

TOMATO-CURRY LENTIL STEW
Servings: 2 | Prep: 10m | Cooks: 50m | Total: 1h

NUTRITION FACTS

Calories: 206 | Carbohydrates: 36.9g | Fat: 0.8g | Protein: 13.7g | Cholesterol: 0mg

INGREDIENTS

- 1/2 cup dry lentils
- 1/4 teaspoon curry powder
- 1 cup water
- 3 cloves garlic, minced
- 5 ounces stewed tomatoes
- salt to taste
- 1/8 cup chopped onion
- ground black pepper to taste
- 2 stalks celery, chopped, with leaves

DIRECTIONS

1. Combine lentils and water, bring to a boil.
2. Lower heat to simmer, add tomatoes, onion, and celery. Cover and let simmer 45 minutes. Check every 15 minutes to stir, and add water if necessary. Add spices last 15 minutes to taste. Taste and re-spice if necessary before serving.

TASTY LENTIL TACOS
Servings: 6 | Prep: 10m | Cooks: 40m | Total: 50m

NUTRITION FACTS

Calories: 304 | Carbohydrates: 44.2g | Fat: 10g | Protein: 9.4g | Cholesterol: 1mg

INGREDIENTS

- 1 teaspoon canola oil
- 1 tablespoon taco seasoning, or to taste
- 2/3 cup finely chopped onion
- 1 2/3 cups chicken broth
- 1 small clove garlic, minced

- 2/3 cup salsa
- 2/3 cup dried lentils, rinsed
- 12 taco shells

DIRECTIONS

1. Heat oil in a skillet over medium heat; cook and stir onion and garlic until tender, about 5 minutes. Mix lentils and taco seasoning into onion mixture; cook and stir for 1 minute.
2. Pour chicken broth into skillet and bring to a boil. Reduce heat to low, cover the skillet, and simmer until lentils are tender, 25 to 30 minutes.
3. Uncover the skillet and cook until mixture is slightly thickened, 6 to 8 minutes. Mash lentils slightly; stir in salsa.
4. Serve about 1/4 cup lentil mixture in each taco shell.

VEGGIE BURGERS

Servings: 8 | Prep: 15m | Cooks: 20m | Total: 1h35m

NUTRITION FACTS

Calories: 193 | Carbohydrates: 31.9g | Fat: 4.3g | Protein: 6.9g | Cholesterol: 27mg

INGREDIENTS

- 2 teaspoons olive oil
- 1 1/2 cups rolled oats
- 1 small onion, grated
- 1/4 cup shredded Cheddar cheese
- 2 cloves crushed garlic
- 1 egg, beaten
- 2 carrots, shredded
- 1 tablespoon soy sauce
- 1 small summer squash, shredded
- 1 1/2 cups all-purpose flour
- 1 small zucchini, shredded

DIRECTIONS

1. Heat the olive oil in a skillet over low heat, and cook the onion and garlic for about 5 minutes, until tender. Mix in the carrots, squash, and zucchini. Continue to cook and stir for 2 minutes. Remove pan from heat, and mix in oats, cheese, and egg. Stir in soy sauce, transfer the mixture to a bowl, and refrigerate 1 hour.
2. Preheat the grill for high heat.
3. Place the flour on a large plate. Form the vegetable mixture into eight 3 inch round patties. Drop each patty into the flour, lightly coating both sides.
4. Oil the grill grate, and grill patties 5 minutes on each side, or until heated through and nicely browned.

WINTER CHICKEN BAKE

Servings: 2 | Prep: 25m | Cooks: 55m | Total: 1h20m

NUTRITION FACTS

Calories: 319 | Carbohydrates: 46.3g | Fat: 2g | Protein: 29.8g | Cholesterol: 68mg

INGREDIENTS

- 1 sweet potato
- 2 skinless, boneless chicken breast halves
- 1/2 medium sweet onion, chopped
- 2 tablespoons barbecue sauce
- 1 medium apple - peeled, cored, and chopped
- 1 cup cranberries
- 3 carrots, peeled and chopped

DIRECTIONS

1. Preheat oven to 375 degrees F (190 degrees C). Lightly grease a baking dish.
2. Pierce the sweet potato several times with a fork and cut in half. Place in a microwave-safe dish; pour water to about 1/2-inch deep. Cook in microwave 10 minutes.
3. Arrange the onion, apple, and carrots into the bottom of the prepared baking dish. Brush the barbecue sauce on both sides of the chicken breasts and lay atop the vegetables. Peel the sweet potato and cut into large chunks; scatter into the baking dish. Sprinkle the cranberries over the dish.
4. Bake in the preheated oven until the chicken is tender and no longer pink in the center, 45 to 55 minutes. Allow to cool 5 minutes before serving.

BEST EVER SPLIT PEA

Servings: 8 | Prep: 20m | Cooks: 2h30m | Total: 2h50m

NUTRITION FACTS

Calories: 133 | Carbohydrates: 18.4g | Fat: 2.1g | Protein: 11.2g | Cholesterol: 0mg

INGREDIENTS

- 1 tablespoon olive oil
- 1 cup yellow split peas
- 2 cups chopped onion
- 1 cup green split peas
- 2 cups chopped carrot
- 8 cups fat-free chicken broth

- 2 cups finely chopped celery
- 1 1/2 teaspoons salt-free seasoning blend
- 1/2 tablespoon minced garlic
- 1 teaspoon salt

DIRECTIONS

1. In a large pot or Dutch oven over medium heat, heat olive oil. Cook onion, carrot, celery and garlic until onion is translucent. Stir in yellow and green split peas, broth, seasoning and salt. Cover, bring to a boil, then reduce heat and simmer 2 1/2 hours, stirring frequently. Puree with a blender or food processor. Return to pot, heat through, and serve.

ASIAN ROLL LETTUCE WRAP
Servings: 4 | Prep: 35m | Cooks: 25m | Total: 1h

NUTRITION FACTS

Calories: 369 | Carbohydrates: 42.8g | Fat: 9.9g | Protein: 28.6g | Cholesterol: 84mg

INGREDIENTS

- 1 pound ground turkey
- 1 cup sliced red bell pepper
- 1 tablespoon light soy sauce
- 1 cup sliced radishes
- 1 teaspoon minced garlic
- 1/3 cup light soy sauce
- 2 teaspoons minced fresh ginger root
- 1/3 cup water
- 1 cup brown rice
- 3 tablespoons fresh lemon juice
- 1 cup water
- 2 teaspoons minced garlic
- 16 large lettuce leaves
- 1 tablespoon minced fresh ginger root
- 1 cup shredded carrots
- 1 teaspoon sugar
- 1 cup green onions, thinly sliced

DIRECTIONS

1. In a medium bowl, mix together ground turkey, 1 tablespoon soy sauce, 1 teaspoon minced garlic and 2 teaspoons ginger. Form into 16 meatballs and roll into ovals. Cover and refrigerate.

2. In a medium saucepan over medium heat, combine rice with 2 cups water. Bring to a boil, reduce heat and simmer for 20 minutes, or until rice is tender.

3. Preheat the grill or broiler. Arrange rice, lettuce leaves, carrots, scallions, radishes and red peppers onto a serving platter or place each into a small bowl. In a medium bowl, mix together 1/3 cup soy sauce, 1/3 cup water, lemon juice, 2 teaspoons garlic, 1 tablespoon ginger, and sugar. Divide into 4 small dipping bowls.

4. Thread two meatballs onto each 10 inch skewer. Grill or broil for 10 to 12 minutes, turning occasionally to brown all sides. If broiling, line the broiler pan with aluminum foil and drain fat after 6 minutes.

5. To eat, place a leaf of lettuce onto the palm of your hand, spoon on a little rice, then a meat roll, and a few of the vegetables. Roll up and dip in dipping sauce or spoon sauce over.

SOUTHERN HAM AND BROWN BEANS
Servings: 8 | Prep: 10m | Cooks: 3m | Total: 3h10m

NUTRITION FACTS

Calories: 272 | Carbohydrates: 37.7g | Fat: 6g | Protein: 16.7g | Cholesterol: 17mg

INGREDIENTS

- 1 pound dry pinto beans
- 2 cloves garlic, minced
- 8 cups water
- 1 teaspoon chili powder
- 1 large, meaty ham hock
- 1 teaspoon salt, or to taste
- 1 large onion, chopped
- 1/4 teaspoon ground black pepper, or to taste

DIRECTIONS

1. Place the beans and water in a large stockpot. Add the ham hock, onion and garlic. Season with chili powder, salt and pepper. Bring to a boil, and cook for 2 minutes. Cover, and remove from heat. Let stand for one hour.

2. Return the pot to the heat, and bring to a boil once again. Reduce heat to medium-low, and simmer for at least 3 hours to blend flavors. The longer you simmer, the thicker the broth will become. I like to cook mine for about 6 hours.

3. Remove the ham hock from the broth, and let cool. Remove the meat from the bone, and return the meat to the stockpot, discarding the bone. Adjust seasonings to taste.

MEXICAN BEAN AND RICE SALAD

Servings: 10 | Prep: 20m | Cooks: 1h | Total: 1h20m

NUTRITION FACTS

Calories: 124 | Carbohydrates: 26g | Fat: 1g | Protein: 4.7g | Cholesterol: 0mg

INGREDIENTS

- 2 cups cooked brown rice
- 2 jalapeno peppers, seeded and diced
- 1 (15 ounce) can kidney beans, rinsed and drained
- 1 lime, zested and juiced
- 1 (15 ounce) can black beans, rinsed and drained
- 1/4 cup chopped cilantro leaves
- 1 (15.25 ounce) can whole kernel corn, drained
- 1 teaspoon minced garlic
- 1 small onion, diced
- 1 1/2 teaspoons ground cumin
- 1 green bell pepper, diced
- salt to taste

DIRECTIONS

1. In a large salad bowl, combine the brown rice, kidney beans, black beans, corn, onion, green pepper, jalapeno peppers, lime zest and juice, cilantro, garlic, and cumin. Lightly toss all ingredients to mix well, and sprinkle with salt to taste.
2. Refrigerate salad for 1 hour, toss again, and serve.

SLOW COOKER PUMPKIN TURKEY CHILI

Servings: 6 | Prep: 15m | Cooks: 3h10m | Total: 3h25m

NUTRITION FACTS

Calories: 338 | Carbohydrates: 41.9g | Fat: 9.1g | Protein: 25.1g | Cholesterol: 56mg

INGREDIENTS

- 1 tablespoon olive oil
- 1 (15 ounce) can chili beans
- 1 pound ground turkey
- 1 (15 ounce) can seasoned black beans
- 1 onion, chopped
- 3 tablespoons brown sugar
- 1 (28 ounce) can diced tomatoes

- 1 tablespoon pumpkin pie spice
- 2 cups cubed fresh pumpkin
- 1 tablespoon chili powder

DIRECTIONS

1. Heat olive oil in a large soup pot over medium heat; brown turkey, stirring often, until crumbly and no longer, pink, about 10 minutes. Drain and discard any fat.
2. Transfer turkey to a slow cooker and stir in onions, diced tomatoes, pumpkin, chili beans, black beans, brown sugar, pumpkin pie spice, and chili powder. Set cooker to Low, cover, and cook until pumpkin is tender and has started to break apart, at least 3 hours.

GRILLED CHICKEN BURGERS
Servings: 8 | Prep: 30m | Cooks: 15m | Total: 45m

NUTRITION FACTS

Calories: 486 | Carbohydrates: 104.6g | Fat: 4.7g | Protein: 14.5g | Cholesterol: 23mg

INGREDIENTS

- 1 onion, chopped
- 2 pounds ground chicken
- 2 teaspoons minced garlic
- 1 egg
- 1 red bell pepper, chopped
- 1/2 cup fresh bread crumbs
- 1 cup fresh sliced mushrooms
- 1 tablespoon Old Bay Seasoning
- 1 tomato, seeded and chopped
- kosher salt to taste
- 2 carrots, chopped
- black pepper to taste

DIRECTIONS

1. Preheat an outdoor grill for medium heat and lightly oil grate.
2. Lightly spray a saute pan with cooking or oil spray over medium heat. Saute the onion with the garlic first, then the bell pepper, then the mushrooms, tomatoes and carrots, all to desired tenderness. Set aside and allow all vegetables to cool completely.
3. In a large bowl, combine the chicken and vegetables. Add the egg, bread crumbs and seasonings to taste. Mix all together well and form into 8 patties.
4. Grill over medium heat for 5 to 6 minutes per side, or to desired doneness.

SPICY CHICKEN AND SWEET POTATO STEW

Servings: 6 | Prep: 25m | Cooks: 25m | Total: 50m

NUTRITION FACTS

Calories: 361 | Carbohydrates: 44.1g | Fat: 7.7g | Protein: 29.1g | Cholesterol: 57mg

INGREDIENTS

- 1 teaspoon olive oil
- 1 teaspoon ground cumin
- 1 onion, chopped
- 1 teaspoon dried oregano
- 4 cloves garlic, minced
- 1 teaspoon cocoa powder
- 1 pound sweet potato, peeled and cubed
- 1/4 teaspoon ground cinnamon
- 1 orange bell pepper, seeded and cubed
- 1/4 teaspoon red pepper flakes
- 1 pound cooked chicken breast, cubed
- 1 1/2 tablespoons all-purpose flour
- 1 (28 ounce) can diced tomatoes
- 2 tablespoons water
- 2 cups water
- 1 cup frozen corn
- 1 teaspoon salt
- 1 (16 ounce) can kidney beans, rinsed and drained
- 2 tablespoons chili powder
- 1/2 cup chopped fresh cilantro

DIRECTIONS

1. Heat olive oil in a large pot over medium heat. Stir in onion and garlic; cook and stir until the onion has softened and turned translucent, about 5 minutes. Stir in sweet potato, bell pepper, chicken, tomatoes, and 2 cups of water. Season with salt, chili powder, cumin, oregano, cocoa powder, cinnamon, and red pepper flakes. Increase heat to medium-high and bring to a boil. Dissolve flour in 2 tablespoons water, and stir in to boiling stew. Reduce heat to medium-low, cover, and simmer until the potatoes are tender but not mushy, 10 to 20 minutes. Stir the stew occasionally to keep it from sticking.

2. Once the potatoes are done, stir in corn and kidney beans. Cook a few minutes until hot, then stir in cilantro before serving.

BAKED FALAFEL

Servings: 2 | Prep: 20m | Cooks: 20m | Total: 55m

NUTRITION FACTS

Calories: 281 | Carbohydrates: 39.3g | Fat: 9.3g | Protein: 11.4g | Cholesterol: 93mg

INGREDIENTS

- 1/4 cup chopped onion
- 1/4 teaspoon salt
- 1 (15 ounce) can garbanzo beans, rinsed and drained
- 1/4 teaspoon baking soda
- 1/4 cup chopped fresh parsley
- 1 tablespoon all-purpose flour
- 3 cloves garlic, minced
- 1 egg, beaten
- 1 teaspoon ground cumin
- 2 teaspoons olive oil
- 1/4 teaspoon ground coriander

DIRECTIONS

1. Wrap onion in cheese cloth and squeeze out as much moisture as possible. Set aside. Place garbanzo beans, parsley, garlic, cumin, coriander, salt, and baking soda in a food processor. Process until the mixture is coarsely pureed. Mix garbanzo bean mixture and onion together in a bowl. Stir in the flour and egg. Shape mixture into four large patties and let stand for 15 minutes.
2. Preheat an oven to 400 degrees F (200 degrees C).
3. Heat olive oil in a large, oven-safe skillet over medium-high heat. Place the patties in the skillet; cook until golden brown, about 3 minutes on each side.
4. Transfer skillet to the preheated oven and bake until heated through, about 10 minutes.

SLOW COOKER CHICKEN MOLE

Servings: 6 | Prep: 15m | Cooks: 5h | Total: 5h15m

NUTRITION FACTS

Calories: 289 | Carbohydrates: 28.1g | Fat: 9.2g | Protein: 28.3g | Cholesterol: 59mg

INGREDIENTS

- 1 large onion, chopped
- 1 teaspoon ground cinnamon
- 1/2 cup raisins
- 4 teaspoons chili powder

- 3 cloves garlic, chopped
- 1 teaspoon ground cumin
- 2 tablespoons toasted sesame seeds (optional)
- 1/2 teaspoon ground coriander
- 1 finely chopped canned chipotle chile in adobo sauce
- 1/8 teaspoon ground nutmeg
- 3 tablespoons peanut butter
- 3 tablespoons unsweetened cocoa powder
- 1 (28 ounce) can crushed tomatoes
- 1 1/2 pounds skinless, boneless chicken breasts
- 1 teaspoon sugar

DIRECTIONS

1. Place onion, raisins, garlic, sesame seeds, chopped chipotle pepper, peanut butter and crushed tomatoes in slow cooker. Stir in sugar, cinnamon, chili powder, cumin, coriander, nutmeg, and cocoa powder. Place chicken in the sauce.
2. Cover; cook on Low until chicken is very tender, about 5 hours.

ROASTED GREEN BEANS

Servings: 4 | Prep: 10m | Cooks: 20m | Total: 30m

NUTRITION FACTS

Calories: 101 | Carbohydrates: 16.4g | Fat: 3.7 | Protein: 4.2g | Cholesterol: 0mg

INGREDIENTS

- 2 pounds fresh green beans, trimmed
- 1 teaspoon kosher salt
- 1 tablespoon olive oil, or as needed
- 1/2 teaspoon freshly ground black pepper

DIRECTIONS

1. Preheat oven to 400 degrees F (200 degrees C).
2. Pat green beans dry with paper towels if necessary; spread onto a jellyroll pan. Drizzle with olive oil and sprinkle with salt and pepper. Use your fingers to coat beans evenly with olive oil and spread them out so they don't overlap.
3. Roast in the preheated oven until beans are slightly shriveled and have brown spots, 20 to 25 minutes.

SAVORY KALE, CANNELLINI BEAN, AND POTATO SOUP

Servings: 6 | Prep: 15m | Cooks: 1h | Total: 1h15m

NUTRITION FACTS

Calories: 262 | Carbohydrates: 38.8g | Fat: 5.4g | Protein: 8.2g | Cholesterol: 2mg

INGREDIENTS

- 2 tablespoons extra-virgin olive oil
- 1/2 teaspoon chopped fresh rosemary
- 1 onion, diced
- 1/2 teaspoon chopped fresh sage
- 3/4 cup diced carrot
- 1/2 teaspoon chopped fresh thyme
- 4 cloves garlic, minced
- 1 (16 ounce) can cannellini beans, rinsed and drained
- 3 cups low-sodium chicken broth
- 2 cups finely chopped kale leaves
- 2 cups water
- 1 small red chile pepper, seeded and chopped fine
- 1 cup white wine
- ground black pepper to taste
- 3 potatoes, halved and sliced

DIRECTIONS

1. Heat the olive oil in a large Dutch oven over medium heat; cook and stir the onion until softened and translucent, about 5 minutes. Stir in the carrot and garlic, and cook for 5 minutes more.
2. Pour in the chicken broth, water, and white wine; stir in the potatoes, rosemary, sage, and thyme. Bring to a boil over high heat, then reduce heat to medium-low, cover, and simmer until the potatoes are tender, about 20 minutes. Add the cannelini beans, kale, chile pepper, and black pepper, and simmer, covered, for 30 more minutes.

WINTER LENTIL VEGETABLE SOUP

Servings: 6 | Prep: 20m | Cooks: 1h30m | Total: 3h

NUTRITION FACTS

Calories: 112 | Carbohydrates: 21.9g | Fat: 0.6g | Protein: 6.4g | Cholesterol: 2mg

INGREDIENTS

- 1/2 cup red or green lentils

- 1 clove garlic, crushed
- 1 cup chopped onion
- 1 teaspoon salt
- 1 stalk celery, chopped
- 1/2 teaspoon ground black pepper
- 2 cups shredded cabbage
- 1/4 teaspoon white sugar
- 1 (28 ounce) can whole peeled tomatoes, chopped
- 1/2 teaspoon dried basil
- 2 cups chicken broth
- 1/2 teaspoon dried thyme
- 3 carrots, chopped
- 1/4 teaspoon curry powder

DIRECTIONS

1. Place the lentils into a stockpot or a Dutch oven and add water to twice the depth of the lentils. Bring to a boil, then lower heat and let simmer for about 15 minutes. Drain and rinse lentils; return them to the pot.

2. Add onion, celery, cabbage, tomatoes, chicken broth, carrots and garlic to the pot and season with salt, pepper, sugar, basil, thyme and curry. Cook, simmering for 1 1/2 to 2 hours or until desired tenderness is achieved.

GOOD 100% WHOLE WHEAT BREAD
Servings: 12 | Prep: 5m | Cooks: 3h | Total: 3h5m

NUTRITION FACTS

Calories: 124 | Carbohydrates: 24g | Fat: 1.9g | Protein: 4.7g | Cholesterol: 0mg

INGREDIENTS

- 1 1/2 teaspoons active dry yeast
- 1 1/2 tablespoons nonfat dry milk powder
- 3 cups whole wheat flour
- 1 1/2 tablespoons margarine
- 1 1/2 teaspoons salt
- 1 1/4 cups warm water (110 degrees F/45 degrees C)
- 1 1/2 tablespoons white sugar

DIRECTIONS

1. Place ingredients in the bread machine pan in the order suggested by the manufacturer.
2. Select Whole Wheat or Basic Bread setting. Press Start.

FROZEN VEGETABLE STIR-FRY

Servings: 6 | Prep: 5m | Cooks: 5m | Total: 10m

NUTRITION FACTS

Calories: 88 | Carbohydrates: 13.8g | Fat: 2.9g | Protein: 3.5g | Cholesterol: 0mg

INGREDIENTS

- 2 tablespoons soy sauce
- 2 teaspoons peanut butter
- 1 tablespoon brown sugar
- 2 teaspoons olive oil
- 2 teaspoons garlic powder
- 1 (16 ounce) package frozen mixed vegetables

DIRECTIONS

1. Combine soy sauce, brown sugar, garlic powder, and peanut butter in a small bowl.
2. Heat oil in a large skillet over medium heat; cook and stir frozen vegetables until just tender, 5 to 7 minutes. Remove from heat and fold in soy sauce mixture.

SLOW COOKER BALSAMIC CHICKEN

Servings: 6 | Prep: 15m | Cooks: 4h | Total: 4h15m

NUTRITION FACTS

Calories: 200 | Carbohydrates: 17.6g | Fat: 6.8g | Protein: 18.6g | Cholesterol: 43mg

INGREDIENTS

- 2 tablespoons olive oil
- 1 teaspoon dried basil
- 4 skinless, boneless chicken breast halves, or more to taste
- 1 teaspoon dried rosemary
- salt and ground black pepper to taste
- 1/2 teaspoon dried thyme
- 1 onion, thinly sliced
- 1/2 cup balsamic vinegar
- 4 cloves garlic
- 2 (14.5 ounce) cans crushed tomatoes
- 1 teaspoon dried oregano

DIRECTIONS

1. Drizzle olive oil into the slow cooker. Place chicken breasts on top of oil and season each breast with salt and pepper. Top chicken breasts with onion slices, garlic, oregano, basil, rosemary, and thyme. Drizzle balsamic vinegar over seasoned breasts and pour tomatoes on top.

2. Cook in the slow cooker set to High until chicken is no longer pink in the center and the juices run clear, about 4 hours.

GARLIC CHICKEN FRIED BROWN RICE
Servings: 3 | Prep: 20m | Cooks: 15m | Total: 35m

NUTRITION FACTS

Calories: 444 | Carbohydrates: 57.4g | Fat: 12.8g | Protein: 24.3g | Cholesterol: 43mg

INGREDIENTS

- 2 tablespoons vegetable oil, divided
- 3 cups cooked brown rice
- 8 ounces skinless, boneless chicken breast, cut into strips
- 2 tablespoons light soy sauce
- 1/2 red bell pepper, chopped
- 1 tablespoon rice vinegar
- 1/2 cup green onion, chopped
- 1 cup frozen peas, thawed
- 4 cloves garlic, minced

DIRECTIONS

1. Heat 1 tablespoon of vegetable oil in a large skillet set over medium heat. Add the chicken, bell pepper, green onion and garlic. Cook and stir until the chicken is cooked through, about 5 minutes. Remove the chicken to a plate and keep warm.

2. Heat the remaining tablespoon of oil in the same skillet over medium-high heat. Add the rice; cook and stir to heat through. Stir in the soy sauce, rice vinegar and peas, and continue to cook for 1 minute. Return the chicken mixture to the skillet and stir to blend with the rice and heat through before serving.

INSTANT POT VEGAN CABBAGE DETOX SOUP
Servings: 4 | Prep: 15m | Cooks: 10m | Total: 45m

NUTRITION FACTS

Calories: 67 | Carbohydrates: 13.4g | Fat: 0.4g | Protein: 2.3g | Cholesterol: 0mg

INGREDIENTS

- 3 cups coarsely chopped green cabbage
- 1 onion, chopped
- 2 1/2 cups vegetable broth
- 2 cloves garlic
- 1 (14.5 ounce) can diced tomatoes
- 2 tablespoons apple cider vinegar
- 3 carrots, chopped
- 1 tablespoon lemon juice
- 3 stalks celery, chopped
- 2 teaspoons dried sage

DIRECTIONS

1. Combine cabbage, vegetable broth, diced tomatoes, carrots, celery, onion, garlic, apple cider vinegar, lemon juice, and sage in a multi-functional pressure cooker (such as Instant Pot(R)). Close and lock the lid. Select high pressure according to manufacturer's instructions; set timer for 15 minutes. Allow 10 to 15 minutes for pressure to build.
2. Release pressure using the natural-release method according to manufacturer's instructions, 10 to 40 minutes. Unlock and remove lid.

NORTHERN ITALIAN BEEF STEW
Servings: 8 | Prep: 30m | Cooks: 4h20m | Total: 4h50m

NUTRITION FACTS

Calories: 476 | Carbohydrates: 34.4g | Fat: 10.2g | Protein: 49.9g | Cholesterol: 102mg

INGREDIENTS

- 2 tablespoons olive oil
- 4 large tomatoes, chopped
- 2 pounds lean top round, trimmed and cut into 1-inch cubes
- 1 1/2 pounds red potatoes (such as Red Bliss), cut into 1-inch chunks
- 2 large sweet onions, diced
- 1 tablespoon dried basil
- 2 cups large chunks of celery
- 1 teaspoon dried thyme
- 4 large carrots, peeled and cut into large rounds
- 1 teaspoon dried marjoram
- 1 pound crimini mushrooms, sliced
- 1/2 teaspoon dried sage
- 2 tablespoons minced garlic

- 1 quart beef stock
- 2 cups dry red wine
- 2 cups tomato sauce

DIRECTIONS

1. Heat olive oil in a large skillet over medium-high heat. Cook beef in batches in hot oil until browned completely, about 5 minutes per batch. Remove browned beef cubes to a plate lined with paper towels, keeping skillet over heat and retaining the beef drippings.

2. Cook and stir onion, celery, and carrots in the retained beef drippings until just softened, 2 to 3 minutes. Stir mushrooms and garlic into the onion mixture.

3. Pour red wine into the pan; bring to a boil while scraping the browned bits of food off the bottom of the pan with a wooden spoon. Continue cooking the mixture until the wine evaporates, 7 to 10 minutes. Stir tomatoes into the mixture.

4. Pour red wine into the pan; bring to a boil while scraping the browned bits of food off the bottom of the pan with a wooden spoon. Continue cooking the mixture until the wine evaporates, 7 to 10 minutes. Stir tomatoes into the mixture.

5. Reduce heat to low and simmer until the beef is very tender and the sauce is thick, 4 to 6 hours.

SOUTHWEST WHITE CHICKEN CHILI
Servings: 6 | Prep: 10m | Cooks: 20m | Total: 30m

NUTRITION FACTS

Calories: 323 | Carbohydrates: 36.6g | Fat: 9.4g | Protein: 24g | Cholesterol: 46mg

INGREDIENTS

- 1 tablespoon vegetable oil
- 1 (10.75 ounce) can Campbell's Condensed Cream of Chicken Soup (Regular or 98% Fat Free)
- 4 (4 ounce) skinless, boneless chicken breast halves, cut into cubes
- 3/4 cup water
- 4 teaspoons chili powder
- 1 ½ cups frozen whole kernel corn
- 2 teaspoons ground cumin
- 2 (15 ounce) cans white kidney beans (cannellini), rinsed and drained
- 1 large onion, chopped
- 2 tablespoons shredded Cheddar cheese
- 1 medium green pepper, chopped

DIRECTIONS

1. Heat the oil in a 4-quart saucepan over medium-high heat. Add the chicken, chili powder, cumin, onion and pepper and cook until the chicken is cooked through and the vegetables are tender, stirring often.
2. Stir the soup, water, corn and beans in the saucepan and heat to a boil. Reduce the heat to low. Cover and cook for 5 minutes, stirring occasionally. Sprinkle with the cheese.

GARY'S TURKEY BURRITOS
Servings: 6 | Prep: 5m | Cooks: 20m | Total: 25m

NUTRITION FACTS

Calories: 571 | Carbohydrates: 78.4g | Fat: 7.9g | Protein: 33.8g | Cholesterol: 76mg

INGREDIENTS

- 1 pound ground turkey
- 1 (16 ounce) can fat-free refried beans
- 2 (7.75 ounce) cans Mexican-style hot tomato sauce (such as El Pato)
- 1 (16 ounce) container fat-free sour cream
- 1 (15.25 ounce) can whole kernel corn, drained
- 3/4 cup shredded reduced-fat Cheddar cheese
- 1/2 small onion, diced
- 6 (10 inch) flour tortillas

DIRECTIONS

1. In a large skillet over medium high heat, brown ground turkey. Stir in tomato sauce, corn and onion. Reduce heat to medium and let simmer, stirring occasionally, until liquids reduce (about 20 minutes).
2. In a separate medium skillet, heat beans over medium-low heat. Prepare sour cream and cheese for sprinkling into burritos. One by one, heat tortillas over stove burner for 1 to 2 minutes, flipping a few times. Top with beans, then meat mixture, then sour cream and cheese. Fold over and serve while still warm.

EASY MASOOR DAAL
Servings: 4 | Prep: 5m | Cooks: 30m | Total: 35m

NUTRITION FACTS

Calories: 185 | Carbohydrates: 25g | Fat: 5.2g | Protein: 11.1g | Cholesterol: 0mg

INGREDIENTS

- 1 cup red lentils
- 1/2 teaspoon cayenne pepper, or to taste
- 1 slice ginger, 1 inch piece, peeled
- 4 teaspoons vegetable oil
- 1/4 teaspoon ground turmeric
- 4 teaspoons dried minced onion
- 1 teaspoon salt
- 1 teaspoon cumin seeds

DIRECTIONS

1. Rinse lentils thoroughly and place in a medium saucepan along with ginger, turmeric, salt and cayenne pepper. Cover with about 1 inch of water and bring to a boil. Skim off any foam that forms on top of the lentils. Reduce heat and simmer, stirring occasionally, until beans are tender and soupy.

2. Meanwhile, in a microwave safe dish combine oil, dried onion and cumin seeds. Microwave on high for 45 seconds to 1 minute; be sure to brown, but not burn, onions. Stir into lentil mixture.

ROASTED AND CURRIED BUTTERNUT SQUASH SOUP
Servings: 8 | Prep: 30m | Cooks: 1h10m | Total: 1h40m

NUTRITION FACTS

Calories: 142 | Carbohydrates: 31.1g | Fat: 1.2g | Protein: 4.9g | Cholesterol: 2mg

INGREDIENTS

- 1 butternut squash, halved and seeded
- 1/2 teaspoon dried oregano
- 2 large onions, peeled and quartered
- 1/2 teaspoon ground cinnamon
- 1 medium head garlic
- 1/4 teaspoon ground nutmeg
- 6 cups vegetable broth
- salt and pepper to taste
- 1 bay leaf
- 1 cup plain yogurt
- 1 teaspoon brown sugar
- 1/4 cup chopped fresh parsley (optional)
- 1 teaspoon mild curry powder

DIRECTIONS

1. Preheat oven to 350 degrees F (175 degrees C). Line a baking sheet with parchment paper or aluminum foil.

2. Place squash halves and onion onto the prepared baking sheet. Wrap garlic in foil and set with other vegetables.
3. Roast in the center of the oven for 45 to 60 minutes, until the squash is tender. Remove from oven and set aside until cool enough to handle.
4. Squeeze garlic cloves out of their skin like paste into a food processor. Scrape the flesh from the squash and place into the food processor along with the roasted onion. Puree until smooth. Add vegetable broth if necessary. Transfer the pureed mixture to a stockpot and stir in vegetable broth. Season with the bay leaf, brown sugar, curry powder, oregano, cinnamon, nutmeg and salt and pepper to taste. Bring to a boil and simmer gently for 10 minutes. Remove from heat and stir in yogurt.
5. Remove bay leaf and serve hot. Garnish with fresh parsley if desired.

BAKED SCALLOPED POTATOES
Servings: 8 | Prep: 15m | Cooks: 1h15m | Total: 1h30m

NUTRITION FACTS

Calories: 234 | Carbohydrates: 41g | Fat: 3.3g | Protein: 9g | Cholesterol: 3mg

INGREDIENTS

- 6 large peeled, cubed potatoes
- 1 onion, diced
- 1 (10.75 ounce) can condensed cream of mushroom soup
- 1/2 teaspoon ground black pepper
- 1 1/4 cups milk

DIRECTIONS

1. Preheat oven to 375 degrees F (190 degrees C). Grease a 2 quart casserole dish.
2. Layer potatoes and onions into the casserole dish. Combine soup, milk and pepper in a bowl, then pour soup mixture over the potatoes and onions. The soup mixture should almost cover the potatoes and onion, if it does not add extra milk.
3. Cover dish and bake in preheated 375 degrees F (190 degrees C) oven for 60 minutes or until the potatoes are cooked through. At 30 minutes, remove the casserole from the oven and stir once before returning the dish to the oven. Remove from oven and serve.

RUSSIAN BLACK BREAD
Servings: 12 | Prep: 15m | Cooks: 3h | Total: 3h15m

NUTRITION FACTS

Calories: 69 | Carbohydrates: 11.9g | Fat: 2.2g | Protein: 1.4g | Cholesterol: 0mg

INGREDIENTS

- 1 1/2 cups water
- 1 tablespoon brown sugar
- 2 tablespoons cider vinegar
- 3 tablespoons unsweetened cocoa powder
- 2 1/2 cups bread flour
- 1 teaspoon instant coffee granules
- 1 cup rye flour
- 1 tablespoon caraway seed
- 1 teaspoon salt
- 1/4 teaspoon fennel seed (optional)
- 2 tablespoons margarine
- 2 teaspoons active dry yeast
- 2 tablespoons dark corn syrup

DIRECTIONS

1. Place ingredients into the bread machine in order suggested by the manufacturer.
2. Use the whole wheat, regular crust setting.
3. After the baking cycle ends, remove bread from pan, place on a cake rack, and allow to cool for 1 hour before slicing.

SWEET POTATO GNOCCHI

Servings: 4 | Prep: 30m | Cooks: 35m | Total: 1h5m

NUTRITION FACTS

Calories: 346 | Carbohydrates: 71.1g | Fat: 2.1g | Protein: 9.9g | Cholesterol: 46mg

INGREDIENTS

- 2 (8 ounce) sweet potatoes
- 1/2 teaspoon ground nutmeg
- 1 clove garlic, pressed
- 1 egg
- 1/2 teaspoon salt
- 2 cups all-purpose flour

DIRECTIONS

1. Preheat the oven to 350 degrees F (175 degrees C). Bake sweet potatoes for 30 minutes, or until soft to the touch. Remove from the oven, and set aside to cool.

2. Once the potatoes are cool enough to work with, remove the peels, and mash them, or press them through a ricer into a large bowl. Blend in the garlic, salt, nutmeg, and egg. Mix in the flour a little at a time until you have soft dough. Use more or less flour as needed.

3. Bring a large pot of lightly salted water to a boil. While you wait for the water, make the gnocchi. On a floured surface, roll the dough out in several long snakes, and cut into 1-inch sections. Drop the pieces into the boiling water, and allow them to cook until they float to the surface. Remove the floating pieces with a slotted spoon, and keep warm in a serving dish. Serve with butter or cream sauce.

BEEZIE'S BLACK BEAN SOUP
Servings: 10 | Prep: 1h | Cooks: 5h | Total: 6h

NUTRITION FACTS

Calories: 231 | Carbohydrates: 43.4g | Fat: 1.2g | Protein: 12.6g | Cholesterol: 0mg

INGREDIENTS

- 1 pound dry black beans
- 1 (28 ounce) can peeled and diced tomatoes
- 1 1/2 quarts water
- 2 tablespoons chili powder
- 1 carrot, chopped
- 2 teaspoons ground cumin
- 1 stalk celery, chopped
- 1/2 teaspoon dried oregano
- 1 large red onion, chopped
- 1/2 teaspoon ground black pepper
- 6 cloves garlic, crushed
- 3 tablespoons red wine vinegar
- 2 green bell peppers, chopped
- 1 tablespoon salt
- 2 jalapeno pepper, seeded and minced
- 1/2 cup uncooked white rice
- 1/4 cup dry lentils

DIRECTIONS

1. In a large pot over medium-high heat, place the beans in three times their volume of water. Bring to a boil, and let boil 10 minutes. Cover, remove from heat and let stand 1 hour. Drain, and rinse.
2. In a slow cooker, combine soaked beans and 1 1/2 quarts fresh water. Cover, and cook for 3 hours on High.

3. Stir in carrot, celery, onion, garlic, bell peppers, jalapeno pepper, lentils, and tomatoes. Season with chili powder, cumin, oregano, black pepper, red wine vinegar, and salt. Cook on Low for 2 to 3 hours. Stir the rice into the slow cooker in the last 20 minutes of cooking.

4. Puree about half of the soup with a blender or food processor, then pour back into the pot before serving.

CHICKEN CACCIATORE IN A SLOW COOKER

Servings: 4 | Prep: 10m | Cooks: 6h | Total: 6h10m

NUTRITION FACTS

Calories: 364 | Carbohydrates: 42g | Fat: 8.5g | Protein: 30.8g | Cholesterol: 69mg

INGREDIENTS

- 4 skinless, boneless chicken breast halves
- 3 tablespoons minced garlic
- 1 (28 ounce) jar spaghetti sauce (such as Classico Cabernet Marinara with Herbs)
- 1 1/2 teaspoons dried oregano
- 1 (6 ounce) can tomato paste
- 1/2 teaspoon dried basil
- 1/4 pound sliced fresh mushrooms
- 1/2 teaspoon ground black pepper
- 1/2 yellow onion, minced
- 1/4 teaspoon red pepper flakes (optional)
- 1/2 green bell pepper, seeded and diced

DIRECTIONS

1. Place chicken in a slow cooker; stir in spaghetti sauce, tomato paste, mushrooms, onion, bell pepper, garlic, oregano, basil, black pepper, and red pepper flakes. Cover.

2. Cook on Low until chicken is tender, 6 to 8 hours.

GOBI ALOO (INDIAN STYLE CAULIFLOWER WITH POTATOES)

Servings: 4 | Prep: 15m | Cooks: 20m | Total: 35m

NUTRITION FACTS

Calories: 135 | Carbohydrates: 23.1g | Fat: 4g | Protein: 4g | Cholesterol: 0mg

INGREDIENTS

- 1 tablespoon vegetable oil

- 1/2 teaspoon paprika
- 1 teaspoon cumin seeds
- 1 teaspoon ground cumin
- 1 teaspoon minced garlic
- 1/2 teaspoon garam masala
- 1 teaspoon ginger paste
- salt to taste
- 2 medium potatoes, peeled and cubed
- 1 pound cauliflower
- 1/2 teaspoon ground turmeric
- 1 teaspoon chopped fresh cilantro

DIRECTIONS

1. Heat the oil in a medium skillet over medium heat. Stir in the cumin seeds, garlic, and ginger paste. Cook about 1 minute until garlic is lightly browned. Add the potatoes. Season with turmeric, paprika, cumin, garam masala, and salt. Cover and continue cooking 5 to 7 minutes stirring occasionally.
2. Mix the cauliflower and cilantro into the saucepan. Reduce heat to low and cover. Stirring occasionally, continue cooking 10 minutes, or until potatoes and cauliflower are tender.

KIKI'S BORRACHO (DRUNKEN) BEANS
Servings: 12 | Prep: 30m | Cooks: 3h | Total: 3h30m

NUTRITION FACTS

Calories: 181 | Carbohydrates: 31.8g | Fat: 1g | Protein: 9.6g | Cholesterol: 1mg

INGREDIENTS

- 1 pound dried pinto beans, washed
- 1 white onion, diced
- 2 quarts chicken stock
- 1/4 cup pickled jalapeno peppers
- 1 tablespoon salt
- 6 cloves garlic, chopped
- 1/2 tablespoon ground black pepper
- 3 bay leaves
- 1 (12 fluid ounce) can or bottle dark beer
- 1 1/2 tablespoons dried oregano
- 2 (14.5 ounce) cans chopped stewed tomatoes
- 1 1/2 cups chopped fresh cilantro

DIRECTIONS

1. Soak beans in a large pot of water overnight.
2. Drain beans, and refill the pot with chicken stock and enough water to cover the beans with 2 inches of liquid. Season with salt and pepper. Cover, and bring to a boil. Reduce heat to medium-low, cover, and cook for 1 1/2 hours. Stir the beans occasionally through out the entire cooking process to make sure they do not burn or stick to the bottom of the pot.
3. Stir beer, tomatoes, onion, jalapeno peppers, garlic, bay leaves, oregano, and cilantro into the beans. Continue to cook uncovered for 1 hour, or until beans are tender.
4. With a potato masher, crush the beans slightly to thicken the bean liquid. Adjust the seasonings with salt and pepper to taste.

CUBAN BEANS AND RICE
Servings: 6 | Prep: 10m | Cooks: 50m | Total: 1h

NUTRITION FACTS

Calories: 258 | Carbohydrates: 49.3g | Fat: 3.2g | Protein: 7.3g | Cholesterol: 2mg

INGREDIENTS

- 1 tablespoon olive oil
- 1 teaspoon salt
- 1 cup chopped onion
- 4 tablespoons tomato paste
- 1 green bell pepper, chopped
- 1 (15.25 ounce) can kidney beans, drained with liquid reserved
- 2 cloves garlic, minced
- 1 cup uncooked white rice

DIRECTIONS

1. Heat oil in a large saucepan over medium heat. Saute onion, bell pepper and garlic. When onion is translucent add salt and tomato paste. Reduce heat to low and cook 2 minutes. Stir in the beans and rice.
2. Pour the liquid from the beans into a large measuring cup and add enough water to reach a volume of 2 1/2 cups; pour into beans. Cover and cook on low for 45 to 50 minutes, or until liquid is absorbed and rice is cooked.

SPICY AFRICAN YAM SOUP
Servings: 4 | Prep: 10m | Cooks: 30m | Total: 40m

NUTRITION FACTS

Calories: 345 | Carbohydrates: 62.2g | Fat: 6.9g | Protein: 11.5g | Cholesterol: 0mg

INGREDIENTS

- 1 teaspoon vegetable oil
- 1/2 teaspoon ground cumin
- 1 small onion, chopped
- 1 cup chunky salsa
- 1 large sweet potato, peeled and diced
- 1 (15.5 ounce) can garbanzo beans, drained
- 1 clove garlic, minced
- 1 cup diced zucchini
- 4 cups chicken broth
- 1/2 cup cooked rice
- 1 teaspoon dried thyme
- 2 tablespoons creamy peanut butter

DIRECTIONS

1. Heat the oil in a stockpot over medium heat. Saute onion, sweet potato, and garlic until onion is soft. Turn down heat if necessary to prevent burning.
2. Stir in the chicken broth, thyme and cumin. Bring to a boil, cover and simmer for about 15 minutes. Stir in salsa, garbanzo beans and zucchini. Simmer until tender, about 15 minutes.
3. Stir in the cooked rice and peanut butter until the peanut butter has dissolved. Serve hot with pita chips and a green salad.

HEALTHIER OVEN ROASTED POTATOES
Servings: 4 | Prep: 15m | Cooks: 20m | Total: 35m

NUTRITION FACTS

Calories: 319 | Carbohydrates: 65.5g | Fat: 3.8g | Protein: 7.7g | Cholesterol: 0mg

INGREDIENTS

- 1 tablespoon olive oil
- 1 tablespoon chopped fresh parsley
- 1 tablespoon minced garlic
- 1/2 teaspoon red pepper flakes
- 1 tablespoon chopped fresh basil
- 1/2 teaspoon salt
- 1 tablespoon chopped fresh rosemary
- 4 large potatoes, peeled and cubed

DIRECTIONS

1. Preheat oven to 475 degrees F (245 degrees C).
2. Combine oil, garlic, basil, rosemary, parsley, red pepper flakes, and salt in a large bowl. Toss in potatoes until evenly coated. Place potatoes in a single layer on a roasting pan or baking sheet.
3. Roast in preheated oven, turning occasionally, until potatoes are brown on all sides, 20 to 30 minutes.

BREAD MACHINE PUMPERNICKEL BREAD
Servings: 12 | Prep: 10m | Cooks: 3h45m | Total: 3h55m

NUTRITION FACTS

Calories: 88 | Carbohydrates: 19.6g | Fat: 1.3g | Protein: 1.6g | Cholesterol: 0mg**INGREDIENTS**

- 1 1/8 cups warm water
- 11/2 cups bread flour
- 1 1/2 tablespoons vegetable oil
- 1 cup rye flour
- 1/3 cup molasses
- 1 cup whole wheat flour
- 3 tablespoons cocoa
- 1 1/2 tablespoons vital wheat gluten (optional)
- 1 tablespoon caraway seed (optional)
- 2 1/2 teaspoons bread machine yeast
- 1 1/2 teaspoons salt

DIRECTIONS

1. Place ingredients in the pan of the bread machine in the order recommended by the manufacturer. Select Basic cycle; press Start.

BLACK BEAN AND CORN SALAD
Servings: 6 | Prep: 15m | Cooks: 12h | Total: 12h15m

NUTRITION FACTS

Calories: 304 | Carbohydrates: 49.5g | Fat: 8.5g | Protein: 11.7g | Cholesterol: 0mg

INGREDIENTS

- 1/2 cup balsamic vinaigrette salad dressing
- 2 (15 ounce) cans black beans, rinsed and drained
- 1/4 teaspoon seasoned pepper
- 2 (15 ounce) cans whole kernel corn, drained

- 1/4 teaspoon dried cilantro
- 1/2 cup chopped onion
- 1/8 teaspoon ground cayenne pepper
- 1/2 cup chopped green onions
- 1/4 teaspoon ground cumin
- 1/2 cup red bell pepper, chopped

DIRECTIONS

1. In a small bowl, mix together vinaigrette, seasoned pepper, cilantro, cayenne pepper, and cumin. Set dressing aside.
2. In a large bowl, stir together beans, corn, onion, green onions, and red bell pepper. Toss with dressing. Cover, and refrigerate overnight. Toss again before serving.

BLACK BEAN SALSA
Servings: 6 | Prep: 10m | Cooks: 35m | Total: 45m

NUTRITION FACTS

Calories: 275 | Carbohydrates: 42.3g | Fat: 3.1g | Protein: 20.8g | Cholesterol: 61mg

INGREDIENTS

- 3 skinless, boneless chicken breast halves
- 1 medium head cabbage, shredded
- 8 cups chicken broth
- 1 (8 ounce) package uncooked egg noodles
- 2 leeks, sliced
- 1 teaspoon Thai chile sauce
- 6 carrots, cut into 1 inch pieces

DIRECTIONS

1. Place chicken breasts and broth in to a stockpot or Dutch oven. Bring to a boil and let simmer for about 20 minutes, or until chicken is cooked through. Remove the chicken from the broth and set aside to cool.
2. Put the leeks and carrots into the pot and simmer them for 10 minutes, or until tender. Shred the cooled chicken in to bite sized pieces and return it to the pot. Add the cabbage and egg noodles and cook another 5 minutes or until the noodles are soft. The soup should be thick like a stew. Serve hot and flavor to taste with Thai chili sauce.

BAKED SWEET POTATOES WITH GINGER AND HONEY

Servings: 12 | Prep: 15m | Cooks: 40m | Total: 55m

NUTRITION FACTS

Calories: 162 | Carbohydrates: 34.9g | Fat: 2.3g | Protein: 1.9g | Cholesterol: 0mg

INGREDIENTS

- 3 pounds sweet potatoes, peeled and cubed
- 2 tablespoons walnut oil
- 1/2 cup honey
- 1 teaspoon ground cardamom
- 3 tablespoons grated fresh ginger
- 1/2 teaspoon ground black pepper

DIRECTIONS

1. Preheat oven to 400 degrees F (200 degrees C).
2. In a large bowl, toss together the sweet potatoes, honey, ginger, walnut oil, cardamom, and pepper. Transfer to a large cast iron frying pan.
3. Bake for 20 minutes in the preheated oven. Stir the potatoes to expose the pieces from the bottom of the pan. Bake for another 20 minutes, or until the sweet potatoes are tender and caramelized on the outside.

TOMATO SOUP

Servings: 6 | Prep: 30m | Cooks: 30m | Total: 1h

NUTRITION FACTS

Calories: 141 | Carbohydrates: 26.5g | Fat: 3.4g | Protein: 5.4g | Cholesterol: 0mg

INGREDIENTS

- 1 tablespoon vegetable oil
- 3 1/2 cups vegetable broth
- 1 cup chopped onion
- 1 tablespoon vegetarian Worcestershire sauce
- 2 cloves garlic, minced
- 1 teaspoon salt
- 1/2 cup chopped carrot
- 1/2 teaspoon dried thyme
- 1/4 cup chopped celery
- 1/2 teaspoon ground black pepper

- 2 (28 ounce) cans crushed tomatoes
- 4 drops hot pepper sauce

DIRECTIONS

1. Heat oil in a large Dutch oven over medium-high heat. Saute onion and garlic until onion is tender.
2. Add carrot and celery; cook 7 to 9 minutes until tender, stirring frequently. Stir in tomatoes, broth, Worcestershire sauce, salt, thyme, pepper and hot pepper sauce. Reduce heat to low. Cover and simmer 20 minutes, stirring frequently.

EASY PASTA FAGIOLI

Servings: 4 | Prep: 15m | Cooks: 10m | Total: 45m

NUTRITION FACTS

Calories: 338 | Carbohydrates: 60.7g | Fat: 5.1g | Protein: 13.4g | Cholesterol: 2mg

INGREDIENTS

- 1 tablespoon olive oil
- 1 (14 ounce) can chicken broth
- 1 carrot, diced
- freshly ground black pepper to taste
- 1 stalk celery, diced
- 1 tablespoon dried parsley
- 1 thin slice onion, diced
- 1/2 tablespoon dried basil leaves
- 1/2 teaspoon chopped garlic
- 1 (15 ounce) can cannellini beans, drained and rinsed
- 4 (8 ounce) cans tomato sauce
- 1 1/2 cups ditalini pasta

DIRECTIONS

1. Heat olive oil in a saucepan over medium heat. Saute carrot, celery and onion until soft. Add garlic and saute briefly. Stir in tomato sauce, chicken broth, pepper, parsley and basil; simmer for 20 minutes.
2. Bring a large pot of lightly salted water to a boil. Add ditalini pasta and cook for 8 minutes or until al dente; drain.
3. Add beans to the sauce mixture and simmer for a few minutes. When pasta is done, stir into sauce and bean mixture.

PASTA FAGIOLI SOUP

Servings: 8 | Prep: 15m | Cooks: 1h | Total: 1h15m

NUTRITION FACTS

Calories: 256 | Carbohydrates: 48.4g | Fat: 1.1g | Protein: 13.5g | Cholesterol: 0mg

INGREDIENTS

- 1 (29 ounce) can diced tomatoes
- 8 slices crisp cooked bacon, crumbled
- 2 (14 ounce) cans great Northern beans, undrained
- 1 tablespoon dried parsley
- 1 (14 ounce) can chopped spinach, drained
- 1 teaspoon garlic powder
- 2 (14.5 ounce) cans chicken broth
- 1 1/2 teaspoons salt
- 1 (8 ounce) can tomato sauce
- 1/2 teaspoon ground black pepper
- 3 cups water
- 1/2 teaspoon dried basil
- 1 tablespoon minced garlic
- 1/2 pound seashell pasta

DIRECTIONS

1. In a large stock pot, combine diced tomatoes, beans, spinach, chicken broth, tomato sauce, water, garlic, bacon, parsley, garlic powder, salt, pepper, and basil. Bring to a boil, and let simmer for 40 minutes, covered.

2. Add pasta and cook uncovered until pasta is tender, approximately 10 minutes. Ladle soup into individual serving bowls, sprinkle cheese on top, and serve.

DAIRY FREE CHOCOLATE PUDDING

Servings: 2 | Prep: 10m | Cooks: 10m | Total: 45m

NUTRITION FACTS

Calories: 267 | Carbohydrates: 53.3g | Fat: 4.7g | Protein: 8.1g | Cholesterol: 0mg

INGREDIENTS

- 3 tablespoons cornstarch
- 1/4 teaspoon vanilla extract
- 2 tablespoons water
- 1/4 cup white sugar
- 1 1/2 cups soy milk
- 1/4 cup unsweetened cocoa powder

DIRECTIONS

1. In small bowl, combine cornstarch and water to form a paste.

2. In large saucepan over medium heat, stir together soy milk, vanilla, sugar, cocoa and cornstarch mixture. Cook, stirring constantly, until mixture boils. Continue to cook and stir until mixture thickens. Remove from heat. Pudding will continue to thicken as it cools. Allow to cool five minutes, then chill in refrigerator until completely cool.

POLLO (CHICKEN) FRICASSEE FROM PUERTO RICO
Servings: 4 | Prep: 40m | Cooks: 6h | Total: 6h40m

NUTRITION FACTS

Calories: 643 | Carbohydrates: 85.2g | Fat: 17.9g | Protein: 32.7g | Cholesterol: 92mg

INGREDIENTS

- 1 pound chicken drumsticks
- 5 cloves garlic, minced
- 1 tablespoon adobo seasoning
- 1 bunch fresh cilantro, chopped
- 1/2 (.18 ounce) packet sazon seasoning
- 2 tablespoons olive oil
- 1/2 teaspoon salt
- 1/2 cup dry red wine
- 5 large red potatoes, peeled and thickly sliced
- 1 teaspoon ground cumin
- 1 large red bell pepper, seeded and chopped
- 1 teaspoon dried oregano
- 1 large green bell pepper, seeded and chopped
- 2 fresh or dried bay leaves
- 1 large onion, chopped

DIRECTIONS

1. Wash the chicken and pat dry; place into a large bowl. Season with adobo seasoning, sazon seasoning, and salt. Place the legs into a slow cooker, and cover with the potato slices.

2. Puree the red pepper, green pepper, onion, garlic, cilantro, olive oil, wine, cumin, and oregano in a blender. Pour over the chicken and add the bay leaves.

3. Cook on Low for 6 to 8 hours, until the chicken is easily removed from the bone.

CALIFORNIA SHERRY CHICKEN

Servings: 4 | Prep: 10m | Cooks: 20m | Total: 30m

NUTRITION FACTS

Calories: 301 | Carbohydrates: 26.5g | Fat: 7.8g | Protein: 30.6g | Cholesterol: 72mg

INGREDIENTS

- 4 skinless, boneless chicken breast halves
- 1/2 cup chicken broth
- 1/4 cup all-purpose flour
- 1 clove garlic, minced
- 1 teaspoon salt
- 1/2 lemon
- 1 teaspoon ground black pepper
- 4 carrots
- 1 tablespoon olive oil
- 4 zucchini squashes, julienned
- 1/2 cup cooking sherry

DIRECTIONS

1. Place chicken in a resealable plastic bag with flour, salt, and pepper. Seal bag and shake to coat. Remove chicken from bag, shaking off excess flour.
2. Heat oil in a large skillet over medium high heat. Brown chicken on each side for about 5 minutes, or until golden. Remove from skillet and set aside.
3. In same skillet combine sherry, broth, garlic and a squeeze of lemon and bring to a boil. Return chicken to skillet, reduce heat to low and simmer for 15 to 20 minutes, or until chicken is cooked through and no longer pink inside.
4. In the meantime, saute carrots and zucchini in a separate medium skillet until they are tender. Add to simmering chicken and sauce and heat through before serving.

Printed in Great Britain
by Amazon

44416911R00059